New and Collected Poems

Robert Conques

First published in 1988 by Century Hutchinson Ltd, Brookmount
House, 62–65 Chandos Place, Covent Garden, London WC2N 4NW

Century Hutchinson Publishing Group (Australia) Pty Ltd
16–22 Church Street, Hawthorn, Melbourne, Victoria 3122

Century Hutchinson Group (NZ) Ltd
32–34 View Road, PO Box 40-086, Glenfield, Auckland 10

Century Hutchinson Group (SA) Pty Ltd
PO Box 337, Bergvlei 2012, South America

ISBN 0 09 173556 4

Printed in Great Britain

for

LIDDIE

Acknowledgments are due to Macmillan and co, Hutchinson and co, Chatto and Windus Ltd, Maurice Temple Smith Ltd, London; and St Martin's Press, Macmillan Inc, New York and Buckabest Books, Menlo Park; also to *London Magazine, The Listener, The New Statesman, The Spectator, The Times Literary Supplement, Tribune, Stand, P N Review, Twentieth Century Verse, The New Humanist, Listen, The Book of the PEN, Botteghe Oscure, Poetry Northwest, The Beloit Poetry Journal, The Times Higher Educational Supplement, Time and Tide, World Review, Encounter, Outposts, Wave, The Observer, The Vanderbilt Poetry Review, Moments of Truth* and the Poem of the Month Club, which first published most of these poems.

NOTE

These poems are not given in their order of original periodical publication; and even that was not necessarily the order of their composition : for example ' For the Death of a Poet ', though written in 1944, was only published in 1950. In the collections of shorter poems there are a number which, though appearing in magazines before earlier collections, were for various reasons postponed from book to book ; so that each such section contains earlier, sometimes much earlier, work.

Although this is a ' collected ' poems, it is not ' complete ' . Some very recent published poems have been omitted, as have (on various grounds) a few dozen previously collected or uncollected.

CONTENTS

from POEMS

TWO ODES

from BETWEEN MARS AND VENUS

from   ARIAS FROM A LOVE OPERA

COMING ACROSS

from THE ABOMINATION OF MOAB

from FORAYS

THE EYE OF THE STORM

Appendix : from REASONABLE RHYMES by Ted Pauker

from POEMS

N a n t u c k e t

It lay in the mist or the wind.

Perhaps Karlsefni saw it to starboard
On the voyage to Hóp from Straumfjord.

Fisherman, farmers and theologians
Settled the swept bay and the crescent bluffs.

And then its attention was filled with whales.
A blunt, chipped sickle : it reaped the sea.
Oh, that was an astonishing empire !
All the oceans gave up to its hunters
Dangerous and profitable monsters.
Folgers and Husseys, Starbucks and Coffins,
Branded the salt wrath with their keels and spears.

Melville chose them, the boldest men on earth,
To be his champions on the demon seas
Of his heart. Even they succumbed.
Ahab died. The waters washed
The ruined survivor to another coast.

The whaling went elsewhere, to techniques and guns.
And the island lies in its parish, weather and past.

Guided Missiles Experimental Range

Soft sounds and odours brim up through the night
A wealth below the level of the eye ,
Out of a black, an almost violet sky
Abundance flowers into points of light.

Till from the south-west, as their low scream mars
And halts this warm hypnosis of the dark,
Three black automata cut swift and stark,
Shaped clearly by the backward flow of stars.

Stronger than lives, by empty purpose blinded,
The only thought their circuits can endure is
The target-hunting rigour of their flight ;

And by that loveless haste I am reminded
Of Aeschylus' description of the Furies :
'O barren daughters of the fruitful night'.

Stendhal's Consulate

He already knows everything that needs to be known.
He has examined his life : his gifts have been shown.
   Immensely capable, he looks from his niche
     Wishing he were reasonably rich.

Reverencing art and love only, still his critique
Does not exempt their instruments or their technique.
   And even in this hot, boring town
     He can still write life down,

Demonstrating what, he feels, must already be plain
To the intelligent and even the sensitive : that life can contain
   A hardness society's verminous power
     May savage but cannot devour.

With evasion and skill he is not wholly separate from
Giulia Rinieri, the music of Mozart, or Rome.
   And with an occasional testing glance
     He continues to watch for his chance.

And his calm gaze penetrates poets' and nations' rage
Expecting us too to be, even in this hot age,
   Fairly resigned to our portions of
     That alloy of failure and love.

Background Music

Summer in Copenhagen ; light on green spires.
Once a philosopher walked beneath these lindens
Thinking : ' Man through imagination enters
The real ; ideas and women are its lures. '

— The life-bound in the sexual act set free
Or in a woman's ambience, split their instants
To quanta from the edge of Time's existence,
And enter the concept of eternity.

Not only that : it gives the landscape form,
And is the immanence of every art.
— Yet though in this green day the idea is yours

It stammers in me to expound in verse
A philosophy deriving from the calm
As you move into the centre of my heart.

Catullus at Sirmio (5 6 B . C .)

At Sirmio, peninsula and island,
It's winter now. The willows are like iron ;
A little snow lies in the furrows ; and mist hides
The far part of the lake's grey shield :
— Not my sort of weather. Light
Comes through the low and heavy sky
With the unequal glare and blur of ice.
Some poet could get beauty out of it, perhaps :
The vaguely outlined mountains, even this blasted wind
Whipping the water.
                          Bring me some hot wine.
This sort of weather's like Caesar,
Single-mindedness with a few cold contrary gusts
— Perversions. I've written about that. He says
I've given him ill-fame for ever. But
He'll get power (if that wet Pompey doesn't)

And then he'll get poets. Still, it's satisfactory
That he minds my cuts : *I* wouldn't. It's the relics
Of shame before the civilized. It'll pass.

Beauty indeed — give me the guts of it — passion ;
And pride if you will. Sweetness I've sought,
The lyrics of simple guiltless lust.
But it was always nonsense. I found the poem
And hid the truth in it ; which was fair enough.
Look at Clodia : breath-taking breasts ;
A green sweat of pleasure ; and my heart whipped
By her bitchiness like this lake by wind — there's beauty !
— But there are worse things : to be frozen
Into the deep black ice of Caesar's epoch.
Oh, they'll fix it. The people want peace and quiet.
They'll back the thug up to dictator ;
If they must have such leaders, let them rot.
Poets will write about victories and buildings,
Tack bits of beauty on to the rulers' conscience
Or do exercises to order about their hearts.

It's a bit warmer.
Noon loosens the water ; the stream flows more freely ;
The trees unstiffen ; the leaves' tongues move and speak.
Beauty, I was saying. Well, what have I got ?
I'll die young and with nothing to show for it
But a few verses and a few brilliant nights
And endless irritation.
— Yet one can't calculate. Timidity and trade
Aren't for Valerians. And I couldn't live in
The ages of disgust ahead. The great make me sick.
Women are whores. And poems ? — it's not as a poet I'm proud.
Still, there may be others of me later. Damn posterity ;
Let *them* read my stuff, if Caesar's boys don't burn it.
In their minds let my pride revel ; and my revenge.

L a k e   S u c c e s s

Fall in Long Island :
Deep in the dying fires of beech and sumach
Under a motionless air holding vapour
Invisible but enough to filter the sun
From a rage of light to a source of clarity,
In these buildings there is talk of peace.

In the Security Council and the six Committees,
In the air-conditioned ambience and too-ideal lighting,
A notoriously maladministered state is smug about mandates,
The sponsor of an aggressor utters pacific phrases,
A state ruled by a foreign marshal condemns colonial oppression,
A middle-easterner makes a statesmanlike speech in very elegant French.

These little men, vain and silly, tough and intelligent, cunning and mean,
Good and patient, selfish and loud, cultured and weak,
Are here distinguished by a different standard of value :
One represents twenty-five thousand tanks,
One speaks with the voice of a whole potential continent,
One has successfully resisted the will of a powerful neighbour,
One of the most impressive is merely an empty voice.

Miles away to the west, high in the air which is
A pale single fluid, the summits of great buildings
Glitter like masked and very distant snow ;
In the foreground, outside the vacant lawns,
Amazingly vivid leaves are slowly falling ;
And in here, in a sense at the heart of the human world,
These tangibles are merely memory,
And paper and words are immediately real. And yet,
In this web of power and propaganda, sufficient
Devotion and intelligence are assembled
To ensure at least a painstaking effort to see
That the chances of peace may not (and that bombs may not)
Fall in Long Island.

The Landing in Deucalion *

Screened by the next few decades from our vision
Their image, none the less, is fairly clear,
Emerging from the air-lock into light
Sharp, unfamiliar in its composition,
From cold stars and a small blue flaming sun
As glints of racing Phobos disappear.

Leaving the rocket pointing at that sky
Their steps and sight turn to the chosen spot
Through this thin air through which the thin winds keen ;
The valves hiss in their helmets as they cross
The crumbling sand towards the belt of green
Where long-sought strangeness will reveal — what ?

And why this subject should be set to verse
Is only partly in what fuels their hearts
More powerful than those great atomic drives
(Resembling as it does the thrust of poetry —
The full momentum of the poets' whole lives)
— Its consummation is yet more like art's :

For as they reach that unknown vegetation
Their thirst is given satisfaction greater
Than ever found but when great arts result ;
Not just new detail or a changed equation
But freshly flaming into all the senses
And from the full field of the whole gestalt.

And so I sing them now, as others later.

* *Deucalionis Regio*, the area to the south of the Sinus Sabaeus, on Mars.

A Woman Poet

The superficial graces go,
And yet such grace remains
About that bare iambic flow
Although the syntax strains
To a tense symmetry, and so
Remotely entertains
    The thundering percussion

Out of the distant heartbeat caught
And never turned away,
Though hidden in a careful thought
No image would delay,
If any image could support
A femininity
    Made flame to purge its vision :

Which saw that fair correcting hand
Resolve the faults of love
In a sweet calculus that spanned
The diapason of
All that a mind could understand
Or mindless music move
    Of passion and compassion.

Near Jakobselv

Dwarf willow, bilberry, bogcotton ; a land of lakes,
And to the north a flat transparent ocean
That stretches to the ice-cap. For those millions
Of frozen tons are always somewhere there,
Though out of sight now and far at the back of the mind
In the long hot day and the green efflorescence.

The insects pipe and drone. The arctic sky,
A very pale blue, completely bare of cloud,
Lays down its haunting midnight on the tundra.
There is no human trace for hours behind us,
And now we lie and sleep, or watch the new

Arctic world that rises like a mayfly
Out of each melting winter and never grows old,
But dies. Nothing here
Is in connexion with the central planet,
With the long histories and the human vision.

Its images are not ours. This speed and brightness
Are innocent of purpose. And in that huge returning
Winter that waits in the north there is no moral
— The ice bears no relation to the anger.
I lie and listen

To the desolating cry of an eagle.
                                        Perhaps
This very newness and this isolation
May strike some hidden tremor in the heart
And make its rock gush water.

                              My companion
Sleeps, scarcely breathing, on the blue-green lichen.
And a faint unchanging radiance plays on us
Out of the whole young landscape, as I lie and watch for hours
The motionless lake and the grebe diving.

The Death of Hart Crane

At first his own effortless high tension
Could match and move the edged electric city,
While under the great bridge sloped the waves,
Flat, tamed, shimmering with oil,
Vestigial to the dying endless sea.

O Queen's, keep off the killing wind.
O Bronx, bring close the seasons and the soil.
O Brooklyn and Richmond, let the sea come through.
And O Manhattan, Manhattan, root and live.

For years the raving city fattened on
Protein of his, as of a million hearts,
But the silent hunger of the sea went on.

Yet if Manhattan by an effort of will
Slowed down for thirty seconds for a prayer
It would no longer be the mindless city
Which, irritating, hurting, driving him to die,
Was none the less his only home.

Blinded at least by neon dawn
He sought the sea with different images,
All the lost galleons and the gazing seals.

But between the Bacardi ports he found that though
The city had too much and meaningless action
The sea had too much death.

A n t h é o r

A heavy light hangs in these silent airs.
Out to the west the failing day prepares
A sultry splendour. Lying on the cliff
I watch the little bay below, the beach,
Red rocks, the slow vibrations of the sea,
Gazing deep into it all as if
    I could find beneath it a truth
    And be free.

What can a poem do with a landscape ? What
Extract that pure philosophies cannot ?
Express the universe in terms of parts
Chosen to illustrate all time and space,

Deducing then beyond those images
The general essence of all human hearts
    And the most transitory look
    On a face ?

The emblems are too crude. The poetry sees
A giant static set-piece where the trees'
Variety shows a single streak of green,
Or overcharged intense cosmographies
Where the light becomes too fluid, spills and soaks,
Washing away the landscape's flickering screen,
    And the hot stars crackle
    In a sky of ice.

Even the parts escape the dying words.
How can they seize precisely on that bird's
White spiral past the bastion of red rock ?
Even the redness is too subtle for
The inexact impressions of a phrase
That draws strength only from the hard-won stock
    Of image flowering from
    Our speech's core.

But word and image, the whole outer song
Can only live as surface to the strong
Thrust of the poet's whole self and language into
Perfection of his knowledge and his life,
Which unintentioned still selects the detail
From sense and vision which may help it win to
    Its own interpretation of
    That hieroglyph.

And yet each day provides its contribution
Of vision to constructing that solution.
And working, upon these red cliffs today,
To let the static and the moving reach
Their place inside one complex of relations,
I find a tentative image in the bay :
    It is the waves of the sea
    On its beach.

Poem for Julian Symons

A not uncommon image nags the verse
(Burke made it grace from dead religions' clash)
— Lacrima Christi from Vesuvius :
Wine out of ash.

Till the excitement of a myth proclaims
Their opposition as the emblem of
Something like the calm of Keats's poems
And the rage of his love.

But I remember, as the image gropes,
That any thirst might relish even more
A vintage pressed out of such gentle slopes
As the Côte d'Or.

For, like all images, this ash-born wine
Is no reliable or fruitful start
For anyone attempting to define
The problems of art.

The Rokeby Venus

Life pours out images, the accidental
At once deleted when the purging mind
Detects their resonance as inessential :
Yet these may leave some fruitful trace behind.

Thus on this painted mirror is projected
The shield that rendered safe the Gorgon's head.
A travesty. — Yet even as reflected
The young face seems to strike us, if not dead,

At least into an instantaneous winter
Which life and reason can do nothing with,
Freezing the watcher and the painting into
A single immobility of myth.

But underneath the pigments' changeless weather
The artist only wanted to devise
A posture that could show him, all together,
Face, shoulders, waist, delectable smooth thighs.

So with the faulty image as a start
We come at length to analyse and name
The luminous darkness in the depths of art :
The timelessness that holds us is the same

As that of the transcendent sexual glance
And art grows brilliant in the light it sheds,
Direct or not, on the inhabitants
Of our imagination and our beds.

A Painting by Paul Klee

O like the shadows now in Plato's cave
The flower throws its outline on the canvas screen
In a grey landscape where each stone
Is as receptive as an eye,
The meticulous petals lying flat and still.

And the sky is calm ; the moon resembles
A glass cave hollowed from the neutral night,
And holds through an agony of silence,
Hearing invisible dust falling,
This bitter fragile lightning and pool of stars.

I see him outline love like an abstract
As with a surgeon's delicacy now
He lays upon the canvas membrane
With a very narrow brush

The coldest colour of the heart.

Dedée d'Anvers

Around the iron bed the camera moves
Or follows where, across the fog-wet stone
She and her life, like one automaton,
Run to exhaustion down the usual grooves.

Quick with desire to glimpse the unobsessed,
It switches restlessly from view to view,
Pauses an instant on a seeming clue ;
Rejects it ; and resumes its nervous quest.

Till in that trajectory of fear and boredom,
Letting the iron twilight slip and slough,
Life burns through briefly to its inch of freedom

And in the flicker of a lens or eye
Forms to one microcosm of all love
A woman's body and her fantasy.

The Classical Poets

Herbert and Vaughan had been able to note in the study
Occasional brilliance that shook through the depths of a soul,
And, later, romantics readily slashed into poetry
The mountain-top flares from hearts made of tinder or coal.

It was different for these : they could energize only by angers
Their clear illustrations of aspects of truth which were well
Understood. Tears would burn through the crystal : to sing about Orpheus
Nor question his motives, who had descended to Hell.

They accepted. They valued the lake at its glittering surface ;
Yet their hearts were too deep. Though they ordered all doubt to disperse
They were poets, and they could not be wholly exempt from its urges
To open the weirs on their taut or magnificent verse.

With descriptions of reason or nymphs or military glory
They corrected the impulse. And, for the whole of their lives,
Like the mermaid on land in the Hans Andersen story,
Pretending to notice nothing, they walked upon knives.

Reading Poetry after a Quarrel

Now the brain's tightnesses unclench
    Into the timeless forms
Where the golden leaf and the snow-bud
Hang from the always-springtime branch.

And that translucence of the best
    Even among its storms
Rebuilds the great impervious dream
On which the world's foundations rest.

Psychokinetic Experiments

The hysteric hears the pin crash to the floor
Two rooms away ; refines his nerves so much
They can be tortured by a feather's touch ;
Or from his thought-split flesh the blood may pour ;

Or Subject A can name the thought-of card
Before that thought has got into a mind :
They cry for systems to be redesigned
Where thought and time break down a logic's guard.

And now, the will diverts the falling dice :
Fresh discords from those future harmonies
Break the experimental frontiers' calm.

And arts may learn that we are back with Kant
Who said he would as little understand
Halting the Moon as moving his own arm.

E p i s t e m o l o g y   o f   P o e t r y

Across the long-curved bight or bay
The waves move clear beneath the day
And, rolling in obliquely, each
Unwinds its white torque up the beach.

Beneath the full semantic sun
The twisting currents race and run.
Words and evaluations start.
And yet the verse should play its part.

Below a certain threshold light
Is insufficient to excite
Those mechanisms which the eye
Constructs its daytime objects by :

A different system wakes behind
The dark, wide pupils till the mind
Accepts an image of this sea
As clear, but in an altered key.

Now darkness falls. And poems attempt
Light reconciling done and dreamt.
I do not find it in the rash
Disruption of the lightning flash.

Those vivid rigours stun the verse
And neural structure still prefers
The moon beneath whose moderate light
The great seas glitter in the bight.

M a t i n g   S e a s o n

Now love and summer hold.
Birds sleep. A distant bell
Informs the fading air
Out of this evening gold.
Yet still the midday's glare
Aches in the failing well.

And now a sunset wind
Shakes sweetness from the trees
And off the stream's surface ;
But blows back in the mind
How the best season suffers
The air's worst agonies.

In March our birds unwinter
Against creative sleets,
But have less strength when this
Close outspoken thunder
Utters its energies
Into the withering heats.

— An image comes that shocks,
So hostile to our love
The purpose it fulfils :
Across the parching rocks
A scorpion stalks and kills
The soft exhausted dove.

H u m a n i t i e s

Hypnotized and told they're seeing red
When really looking at a yellow wall
The children speak of orange seen instead :
Split to such rainbow through that verbal lens
It takes a whole heart's effort to see all
The human plenum as a single ens.

The word on the objective breath must be
A wind to winnow the emotive out ;
Music can generalize the inner sea
In dark harmonics of the blinded heart ;
But, hot with certainty and keen with doubt,
Verse sweats out heartfelt knowledge, clear-eyed art.

Is it, when paper roses make you sneeze,
A mental or a physical event ?
The word can freeze us to such categories,
Yet verse can warm the mirrors of the word
And through their loose distortions represent
The scene, the heart, the life, as they occurred.

— In a dream's blueness or a sunset's bronze
Poets seek the images of love and wonder,
But absolutes of music, gold or swans
Are only froth unless they go to swell
That harmony of science pealing under
The poem's waters like a sunken bell.

A n o t h e r   K l e e

Sliced to a section for the microscope
And stained to fit the habits of the eye,
Which must deduce this sun upon its sky
Circumference to disc and disc to globe,

The shock of art has stopped the moving parts :
The shadow-fish, caught in its needled fins,
Drifts through a sea of unperspectived lines
That cannot be distinguished from its charts.

That cool expanse of unapparent water
Dissolves the stains left by creative violence
And lies untensed along the canvas wove,

But six short lines are locked upon its silence
Seeming an unknown written character
To express what this strange culture means by 'love'.

'Head of a Faun' by Salvator Rosa

With brilliant eyes and quick brown face out-thrust
Against the varnish glaze that holds him far
He leans one moment from the world of legend,
A reassuring and unhurried glimpse
   Pausing between two nymphs
   And unselfconscious lust.
Friendly, uncondescending, self-sufficient
But never breaking into the depths of the heart
He comes to intelligence and gives his message :
'We met once in a brothel or a bar'.
Well, we meet again in what is, after all, art.

A Problem

Liguria tingles with peculiar light.
The sea and sky exchange their various blues.
The asphodel that even goats refuse
   Glows dryly on each rocky height,
Whose foothills' wooded convolutions rise
   Through a heavy, luminous air. And here
   Man might, as well as anywhere,
Combine his landscapes and philosophies.

There Sestri crammed into its littoral shelf
Seems motionless with distance ; motionless
Green flames pour up, the pines and cypresses
   Beyond the stream. The stream itself

Ripples and ripens to a falling sun
   Whose light makes metal at this hour
   Its golden froth of leaf and flower.
A dragonfly is basking on a stone.

Foam spurts between the pebbles ; currents swirl ;
It slides, a shining film, over rock
Smooth as itself, or into pools of dark.
   Where wood and sea and sky and hill
Give static broad simplicities, its course
   At once more complex and more simple
   Appears to thought as an example,
Like the complex, simple movement of great verse.

Gaze in that liquid crystal ; let it run,
Some simple, fluent structure of the all,
No many-corridored dark Escorial,
   But, poem or stream, a Parthenon :
The clear completeness of a gnomic rhyme ;
   .Or, off the beat of pure despair
   But purer to the subtle ear,
The assonance of eternity with time.

How would it come ? This war gave nothing. If
No abstract thought can generate its laws
Unless some special impulse cracks or thaws
   The present icefields of belief :
— Perhaps from the strange new telepathic data,
   Or when the first craft, fairly soon,
   Its rockets flaring, eases down
To total strangeness under Deimos' glitter.

Till then, or till forever, those who've sought
Philosophies like verse, evoking verse,
Must take, as I beneath these junipers,
   Empiric rules of joy and thought,
And be content to break the idiot calm ;
   While many poems that dare not guide
   Yet bring the violent world inside
Some girl's ephemeral happiness and charm.

Poem in 1944

No, I cannot write the poem of war,
Neither the colossal dying nor the local scene,
A platoon asleep and dreaming of girls' warmth
Or by the petrol-cooker scraping out a laughter.
— Only the images that are not even nightmare :
A globe encrusted with a skin of seaweed,
Or razors at the roots. The heart is no man's prism
To cast a frozen shadow down the streaming future ;
At most a cold slipstream of empty sorrow,
The grapes and melody of a dreamed love
Or a vague roar of courage.
                                        No, I am not
The meeting point of event and vision, where the poem
Bursts into flame, and the heart's engine
Takes on the load of these broken years and lifts it.
I am not even the tongue and the hand that write
The dissolving sweetness of a personal view
Like those who now in greater luck and liberty
Are professionally pitiful or heroic. . . .

Into what eye to imagine the vista pouring
Its violent treasures ? For I must believe
That somewhere the poet is working who can handle
The flung world and his own heart. To him I say
The little I can. I offer him the debris
Of five years' undirected storm in self and Europe,
And my love. Let him take it for what it's worth
In this poem scarcely made and already forgotten.

Caserta

Water on bronze postures, a trickle of light
Suggests the slipping arm to the held sight ;
The statues in the fountains are almost moving,
Fauns ready to fall into the groove of loving.

It is a moment, a view from the top of a war.
He became a faun the moment he saw
The nymph immobile in the metal grove.
Her delicate shoulder carries a living dove.

O the slim bronze body can never be woken.
The dove flies. But its myth is not quite broken ;
Though behind it the war is as real as ever,
Is it to be a phoenix to the lover ?

Caught by quick fire in the sharp air's mesh
Can the grace remain in its raw roasting flesh
As in its flight beak, entrail and plume
Historic flames consume ?

A Minor Front

The bridge attributed to Belisarius
Is blown, and we cross the stream on foot
Towards the little town.
                              Absolute power
Has receded like a tide from the Thracian hills
And the people reappears, a streaming rock
Surrounded by dead monsters.
                              Across the Struma
The German outposts can be seen, and their patrols
Still cross the river almost unopposed.
For the retreat was caused by pressure elsewhere
And here no force of partisans can yet
Resist them. Half a dozen towns
Still lie in a no-man's-land which small patrols
Alone can enter.
                              The clouds appear
Fully created in the Aegean sky
And ahead of us the stony and half-empty
Struma glistens.

                        Among the buildings
(Not too badly wrecked) people are moving.
An old man, carrying a wooden bucket
Full of goat's milk, staggers to his neighbour's.
– The quick withdrawal of that violent empire
Has left a vacuum of rule. Government is dead ;
And after the executions by patrols the tired survivors
Learn, for a few days, to work together, to live.
The best are in the mountains with the partisans
Or rotting in Salonika jail. The worst come out
To loot or denounce. And among the others only,
Mediocre and stupid, in small and selfish cities,
Half-suffocated by starvation and disease,
The free life of the holiday camp arises.
Very dimly through a host of more immediate noises
They faintly hear the music of the stateless future
Like a distant waterfall.
                              But there is too much.
Too much confusion ! Too much metal !
They have gazed too long into a mirror of Europe
And seen the Minotaur reflections gnash their teeth,
And they cannot keep their eyes on the green star
Nor listen to the bells.
                              The sky glitters, burning coldly.
The moment is losing its illumination ;
The world of politics and rifles reappears ;
In Seres, Drama, Sidhirokastron, life will revert
To the visionless present.
                              We lower our field-glasses,
And walk back to the far end of the village,
And pull out our rations and begin to eat,
As by the failing light we try to interpret
The gilt inscription on the public monument
In front of which, their hands still tied behind them,
The bodies of two gendarmes lie in the street.

A r i o n

Death and the sea transcended verbal shape.

He gazed at the olive-green unsmooth water, a salt pyre.
To die was more dreadful in his strong imagination,
But through its exalted centre he foresaw an escape.

Oh, the sailors realised the solemnity of the occasion :
Dressed in his ritual clothing, holding the lyre,
He sang an appropriate poem, and when it was done he
Came to the business of the day, was flung in the sea.

No one knows quite what his words were. Fragments of song
Picked up later from sailors in harbourside taverns
Do not sound authentic. And other singers, unfree
For lack of faith or intellectual strength or money,
Have since invented the dolphin for which they all long.

But perhaps as he unhooked his golden collar, ready,
A dolphin on its natural ways, or tempest-driven,
Really appeared and then vanished into the waves
Leaving for a moment an extra streak of foam
To be scattered at once by the splash of his plunging body.

And sailors, and after them poets, made the best of the story
And for ever distorted and fixed the inadequate data
But the truth is : even his corpse was not swept ashore. He,
After a brief agony, sank into calmer water
And with the manuscripts of his best and latest poems
Was rolled by the groundswell through its deepest caves.

On the Danube

(i)

The convicts working on the frontier forts
Have been marched back. The palpable cool air
Of evening lies round me now. A single peasant
Passes unsteadily, reeking of pium brandy,
And then I am alone.
                              The day pauses. The great river
Slides softly by towards the delta and the sea ;
And now the sun strikes from an unaccustomed angle
And the light changes :
                              always at this hour
And in such scenery I wait for revelation,
Under a sky as pale as mother-of-pearl.
It is not that this pure moment can admit
A supernatural vision to the unclear heart,
But it hides the worn planet with its freshness ;
The light is no more absolute, but only
Closer to some untried colour of the air,
And there flickers round the horizons of my heart
The brilliance that precedes a greater brilliance.

(ii)

The winds of Europe and of tragedy
Are filling the sails of poetry here and everywhere.
And I wonder now in what tall uncaused singer
This rich and bitter land warms out.
                                    Last night
In a little inn beside the landing stage
A young man was writing verses at a table
And eating sturgeon stuffed with aubergines.
And perhaps he was the poet for whom the Balkans wait,
Though this is hardly likely.
                              The day before
I saw him reading Marx on a bench beside the river,
The witty laboured blue-prints for perfected anarchy,
Now legal in this country. (The social sky
Holds only now his dialectic for its sun,
But I find a shade by the poetic tree
Under a moon of love.)

Night has fallen,

A young heron rises awkwardly into the air
Under the vague starlight, heading west.
The river ripples as some big fish dives.
And I walk back to the inn.

The moon is rising.

(iii)

I stumble over a machine-gun tripod
Half-buried in the sand. It is now almost eight months
Since the S.S. Regiment 'Turkestan'
Was brought to battle here, surrounded and destroyed,
And a cold complexity of violence still
Lies heavy on this broken continent,
Which these bronze waters and this natural night
Can never answer.

Yet here I am alone and far

From the brilliance of the fighting ideologies,
And I think of a girl in a small provincial town
Looking through a spring rain and imagining love.

Lament for a Landing Craft

Four fathoms under the green
Water, canted between
Two rocks, half on its side
Under the lowest low tide

The flat hull now dimly seen
Bore an armoured machine
Towards the golden wide
Beach, but the forts replied,

Till the swell and the fury were clean
Gone, and it entered a scene
Of soundless shimmer and glide
Heavy with myth. Time died.

And the years' and the waters' sheen
Smoothed out this image, serene
Enough, perhaps, to provide
For eternity's moods, and to guide.

Men escaped, or have been
Made smooth bone by the keen
Teeth. And the weeds hide
Skull, keel, plan, pride.

Sunset under Vitosha

The song tries often to give the true relation
Between the human figure and the face of nature,
To find in the one the other's hidden features.
— It sometimes seems to find an explanation.

But now in the sea-green air and the soft light
It leaves aside your beauty and your kindness,
Its strangeness strikes down through habitual blindness,
Its unknown colours waken and excite.

A sudden absolute silence from the birds,
The sycamore become an orange fire
And every shadow turned to depths of blue :

How can this strangeness shape the whole desire
Into that other beauty which is you ?
What does it mean ? Where are its words ?

Lamartine at Philippopolis

Dawn, pale and hot, came through the Turkish blind.
He opened it and stood and looked at Thrace,
The plain and town conveying to his mind
Such truth as he could draw from fact and place.

Caught like clear water by a curving range
— The blurred rose of Rhodope to the south —
Its very clarity grown strong and strange
The early air came sweetly to his mouth.

Clear light diffused by the outcropping rock
Above the straight Maritza's ochre flow
Entered his heart. And did it there unlock
The politics of fifteen years, and show

The blue and breaking wave on which he soared ;
His songs' clear motives wreck the ancient curse ;
When history gathered to a single chord
And all the rostra spoke heroic verse ?

Or could he in the inn's reviving stink,
The haggling envies rising from the street,
Suspect his gold conceptions' broken link,
The tyrant's pension and the poem's defeat ?

Pliska

History again, but different : the ancient capital
From which Bulgaria draws its age and fullness ;
    The early Khans from here
    Struck their forgotten empire
    Across the Balkan map,
And Krum drank from Nicephorus' gilded skull.

And through a barren nationalism may rant and raise
The giant stones as engines of aggressive war,
    These tombs and temples give
    A real pride and life
    And a felt depth
Beyond the lost five hundred years of Beys.

Their weight can hold that wildness to a fair control
At single points like this, or where, ten miles away,
   History roars from the rocks at Madara
   Where Krum puts a spear through the lion's shoulder
   In a fanfare of inscriptions,
And an ancient honest people becomes a living whole.

A e g e a n

   Sea and evening : in the sky
   Colours of honey, ice and lime.
     I lie in the coastal grove
Of ilexes and cork-trees on the dry
And aromatic ground, relaxed into
My brain and body, not concerned with love.

   Though with you I have often seen
   Occasional objects, branches and stones,
     Glowing with love in your eyes,
Now a more physically haunting dream
Grasps me in this seascape as the summer
Lightning drones around these evening skies.

   Till I am saturated with
   The impersonal magic which long ago
     From women loosed dryads to roam
Through groves like these.
                – In such a sexual myth
You were the first and only one to show me
The relation between a woman and a poem.

Messemvria at Noon

Here is the little building-crowded island
Joined by a narrow causeway to the land ,
Rich brick-reds. and pale browns and whites.

For more than two millennia in this narrow space,
Since the Megarans laid the first foundations,
Houses and churches have been always rising
And falling, like seasonal plants.
                     In the little square
Labourers are digging out the cellars
For some new building. They cut through human strata,
Layers of carved stone and brick, of arch and pillar,
And ghost-talk breaks out from inscriptions
Gagged for centuries. History speaks
With a stone tongue, and also in the gestures
Of fishermen in the little inn repeating
Their ancestors' attitudes and even words.

Back on the mainland now we turn
Where the wind hisses through the sawgrass,
Among scattered light-blue flowers, high up
Among the pale green vegetation of the dunes
And the pale sand, and under a pale blue sky ;
An empty grassland stretches towards the hills,
And far into the distance goes
The long white curve of empty beach
                      And the town
Shines, a concentrate of human living
Set in a desert of natural beauty here.

The heat-haze crystallizes to a prism
Through which we see it clearly, caught in a pale gold
Except for a darkness by the northern cliff
Where the curve of a Byzantine church cupola
Gives from the shadow a single striking light
                    And turning left we see
Far down the bay and visible for miles
The blinding white of a gull.

By Rail through Istria

Limestone and pine : a dry country.
The train curves downhill through the early light
    Towards another day and sea
    That put before the sensitized sight
Complexity that hints of symmetry,
Fit background for the hard thoughts' resolution.
A trace of haze softens the sky's blueness
And this clarity and freshness once again
Present the problem in its old quick newness :
The usual attempt to make perfection plain,
To reduce the world to reason and to poetry ;
    To let the landscape's chthonic impulse
    Flow like a stream to bear the symbols
Through a poem as strictly driven as this train.

    But the poems are waterlogged and lift
Too slowly to the swell of the idea.
    Today I can only begin to clear
    The ground, to note the general drift
Of a poem's necessity. It is not enough
To find a mood to ride the thrust of love,
Nor should the detail of this rock and tree
Fade in a single brilliant light, be lost
In imprecisions of immensity,
Nor golden images proliferate
Except as phosphorescence forming on
    A sea of close secretive strength.
    And by such strictness perhaps at length
I could merge joy with precision ; and create.

    And now we run by the sea,
A streak of blue and shimmer on the shore
    Above which whitish sea-birds soar
    — Specks to an unresolving eye.

And what, for example, is the strict relation
Between the sea which in the last verse figured
As abstract image in a thought's defence,
And this emotive single clear impression
On the visual nerve ; or with the real liquid
Full of weeds and plankton where the fish
Are dumb and the myth-illustrating dolphins
    Grunt, they say, like pigs ? Does some
    Answer pend, or would the poem
Just turn to logic or to gibberish ?

    And now in Monfalcone station
A dark girl, motionless, distracts the heart
From that : its light remembers concentration,
Till single objects fluoresce exact
Radiance to illuminate and illustrate
    The philosophic whole. To sing
    Might flower out of anything :
I learn to seek the fruitful thing or act.

In the Rhodope

The poem tries to speak of the heart
And to relate it to the natural plectrum
Which plucks so clear a note out of its sunlight,
To make its vague, neglected virtues flare
From the ocean and air.

But how does the poem come ?
Its voices bubbling from a pool of darkness
To a deliberate fruit of grapes and peaches ?
Or striking a horror and a melody at night
Down corridors of dead light ?

And how does it distort ?
Like the pearl-diver's hand trembling under water
Towards his stone of food and beauty ? Or
Absolute mirage into a lonely eye
Out of the swan sky ?

— Let me write one more poem,
About this lake at night, black with a golden ice,
Or some green transparent atmosphere at daybreak
Made beautiful by that strange illumination
That poets are always working to bring out
— The colour of doubt.

TWO ODES

For the Death of a Poet

I

I sit alone in the impersonal sunlight ;
Drenched in its pale flame, beside the white waters,
I receive the intense perfection of the heavens,
Complete, serene.

Feeling purely nature's absolute moment,
Passionless melody of revelation
Under a blue and infinitely transparent sky
And wisps of cirrus.

The magnolias shining like white wax, and the dark poplars,
In the sleek meadows the little river gleaming,
And the landscape immaculate and motionless
In the blue heat.

But in this pastoral enchanted air
Sweet with the liquid glitter of Debussy,
Out of a deluge of light your voice speaks to me
Not as for months

Vague and obscurely terrible, in the background,
A note of sadness under all my feeling,
A despairing criticism of every action,
A spoken song,

But clearly stating its case, unanswerably
Putting its claim against the loud avengers
And asking me insistently for at any rate
Some sort of answer.

But how shall I answer ? I am like you,
I have only a voice and the universal zeals
And severities continue to state loudly
That all is well.

Even the landscape has no help to offer.
A man dies and the river flows softly on.
There is no sign of recognition from the calm
And marvellous sky.

Yes, this innocent and sensuous air lies helpless
Above the silky waters. And perhaps your only hope is truly
With me, in all my weakness, and with my tongue that speaks
This ephemeral poem.

II

The afternoon fades subtly across the pine trees
And under a soft and elegiac breeze
The approaching dusk lays down its glowing shadows,

And I think of you there, under the sharp peaks,
In a narrow grave surmounted by a wooden cross,
Emblematic of a faith you did not hold.

I do not deny that on the long view it was worth it,
As one of millions your death paid its expenses —
A half-share in a thirty-yard advance.

Nor can I ask a special treatment for the singer
Who sees the sun's light split through a heart's spectrum
And holds love in his hand like a scalding jewel.

— Yet why was it you and not some self-important fool ?
Why not, for instance, that petty little major
Who in the long run sent you to your death

And now in ease and comfort in America ?
— But how I feel abominably in my heart
Arise the images of disgust and contempt !

— I must put them away. Instead let me hear your poems,
Your young, incomplete, and yet irreplaceable voice
Talking of Doughty or the brass horse. Yes, for years

A few dozen of us will speak and remember
The lines which had to be written, which no one else wrote,
Not overwhelming, not supreme, but unique, a life :

' The dead inside my head are dying of cold '
' Burning in the sky of time like a flare made of fear '
' O strengthen me to number now my heart's Lavals '

Occasionally such words will fall from our speaking brains
To illuminate a spirit's moment or a tongue of love
And reconcile the flesh to its enchanting bells.

— But still, through this golden air, under the clouds'
Mirror of creamy smoke, I ask a reason why you died,
And must the heart's witnesses all stammer and fall silent ?

I listen to the public voice and try to believe it.
I repeat the usual litanies of explanation .
  He died in a good cause ' , ' We sacrifice our best '

' He lives in our memory ' . All this is not untrue
But its irrelevance shakes me like a fever ;
No, they cannot help me, I cannot reconcile

The public need against the private loss,
The just war and the individual's unjust
Death. Cannot admit in fair exchange

The large-scale triumph for the lone disaster,
Or heavens of the future for the present pain.
This is an absolute and total loss

Which no future can ever possible repay.
— I am alone here. The lake shines softly,
Becomes a mirror of mercury, bright and wet.

Down the valley a mist rises, forms like flesh
On the skeleton trees. Upon the towering clouds
The brown sunset carves its colour. And I am alone.

III

Now the world deepens and the dark grows richer ;
A red and mournful splendour fills the eye ;
A sharp sweetness informs the whole of nature,
Holds in a sad, dissolving bliss
Its glories and its agonies.
A golden darkness bleeds across the sky.

Did death perhaps take you with a stunning wonder,
Strange exaltations seize your bursting heart ?
Your face transfigured with passion and splendour
Fade through the absolutely black
Out of the flames of the attack
As the universal harmonies blew apart ?

As on that horrible abyss you trod
Did there walk on across your sea of slaughter
A crucified and all-atoning god,
The aura blazing round its head
Bright as these clouds, as now they spread
Their ample twilight down the crescent water ?

Did some strange call possess you ? Really summon
Heart out of blood-soaked body into pain ?
Death call to you like a woman,
Emerging from that haze of rape
Blood in the air, a liquid shape
Shining in moonlight over all that plain ?

— But I am dazed now by your lost blood's brilliance,
Cannot interpret the flames' halo round your head
Nor see the beauty through that blinding violence
Till clearly, as these splendours die,
There rises through the sad night sky
The awareness of the insulated dead.

IV

Out, high, far out over the night horizon
A bomber's drone recedes into the writhing clouds
And pulls me out of an abyss of sleep. I have been dreaming,

And even now the night still simmers like the nightmare :
The ground sweats, and the sky is thick ; and a raw wind
Rips the edges off all sound and vision, just as when

Below a white air huddled in the dark
The dream drew another eyelid over the sky
And opened a window on a world of ghosts,

Where under a black light I saw your image wander
Into horrible scenes and through disrupted landscapes,
Prey to the hairless monster in the ruined abbey,

Or bleeding to death in a subterranean room
Surrounded by impassive watching faces,
Or endlessly falling down a flames' abyss. . . .

I cannot believe you met a death of passion,
That your ironic individual heart
Could blaze to such a simplifying love ;

Surely you felt only terror and fatigue
Caught in the machinery and champed to a bloody pulp
In the hostile universe's iron mouth,

As the fate that here constructs this violent night
Gave you the message that it yet propounds :
Rupture of flesh and iron, stone and spirit.

And your glorified, transfigured face was only
A bronze mask flung upon you by the sunset :
Really there is only the parching sweat of fear ;

The furred tongue and the headache ; the cold of early morning
Cracking in the knee-joints ; the bowels tight with apprehension ,
And only the will's carapace around the shrinking flesh.

For now the dream can be reassembled :
The assassin shadow moving down its corridors
Be submitted to a close interrogation,

And it says, not pity or regret, but fear. Not only
For you, but for myself. It might have been me,
The dream states, and may be yet : under some slashing barrage

This body and this self may yet be destroyed
In a moment of terror and weakness drop down those cliffs,
Bleed in that room, be crushed in those cold jaws.

— Around me now the sleeping people lie
Inside the glass walls of their thousand nightmares.
An odour of cold corruption from the soil

Hangs in the air. The sky clots into vapour ;
Occasionally shudders with light, splashing phosphorus —
Sudden poisonous flames. The trees shake gently

To distant guns. And a black cold air is pouring
Endlessly from the abyss through which for ever
The outlaw planet pants for sanctuary.

And against the universe I can only put love ;
Against the constellations of despair can only
Give you my hand, and sooner or later die
                                        — Or am I wrong ?

                              V

Midnight : the sky has cleared and the wind ceased.
Behind the motionless poplars now the stars
Shine clear-cut in a very distant sky.
And this meticulous starlight, without mist or eyelid,
Is the only framework for the frozen darkness, its clear
Infrangible bars.

An absolutely naked night whose alien beauty
Contains no element that says ' Rejoice ',
But in the perfect crystal of its sky reveals
— Breaking those engines of the lute and lyre
That claim to speak for us — the quiet image
Of your real voice :

' The world is as it is. There is no helpful answer,
No saving parable or spell that can be told
In blinding rhetorics of star and rainbow.
And the poetry must adorn its indecision
And never can articulate as clearly
As frost or gold.

Out of its decorated and religious dreams
Blaze no despairs or revelations for us both.
Our only hope must be the truly human
Unclearly visible through poetry's mist and dazzle
But shining so brilliantly beneath the inhuman stars :
No angel ; no hero ; but truth.

A cool flame streaming from the brain and body
In which the heart is liberated and possessed ;
Seen as a stubborn muscle working inside a star,
And more than that : felt as a hand,
A fist in the flames or a feather of five fingers
Upon the ripening breast.

Yes, I accept death. I have only the usual regrets.
The individual lives by luck alone.
— But now I must return, under the Italian pines
To stand for ever, while in that crouching sky
There hangs enormously above my fatal valley
The blue moon ' .

And now you have gone : passed through a spirit's violence
Back to the everlasting tryst from which you came,
And only the night's outlandish excellence remains.
I stare up through its brilliance and its distances
While in my charred brain your clear directed voice
Formulates flame.

The river flows across the silence.

                                                        1944.

In the Marshes

Retrospect.
The sunlight filters
Through ten worse years, its categories cooling.
What cannot be reduced to order now
Is irresoluble, life. Let rage or reason take it : —

By a willow, on a narrow bank of moss
And overlooking an almost motionless creek —
The grey-green plain flecked with water
Stretches to a horizonless fading in the distance,
A few mosquitoes whine and a fish leaps —

Ilya is not really in all this, it is
Only a background to a twisting brain,
A symbol of despair like any other landscape.
He is a student. The city and the University
Are far away. The traffic down the Liberation Avenue
And by the National Theatre seems impossible.
The blanketing air contrives to soothe him a little
As he thinks of Stoyanka, lost to him
Probably for ever ; partly his own fault.
He reads the French poet he is trying to translate
But the translation fades into his brain
Or moves impossibly above the non-poetic landscape
And disappears.
                              This is the best season
In the Marshes.
                              In the village the wooden huts
Look almost white under a clear sun,
And the faint haze is slightly luminous around it.
Down in the canal a barge is filled with leather,
The product of the little tannery. The sun is falling.
A flash like a rainbow comes from the oil-tinged mere
In which the abandoned railway breaks and ends ;
Its embankment stretches away eastwards ; it sags in places
And has been entirely washed away in others,
And in one of these the derelict locomotive
Stands like a frozen mammoth in a Yakutsk glacier.
                              Nevertheless, life is lived here.
In a small but handsome house beyond the village
Lives Professor Mantev, former Minister of Trade
And now in exile. The daughter of Tomasin
The dram-shop owner dreams of love. And in a hut
By the canal Pirov the lock-keeper
Holds the secret meetings of the party branch.
There is no gendarme nearer than Shtip, five miles away ;
But the village has suffered several times.

In 1925, in the Civil War
A platoon of legionaries burnt down half the houses
And killed three men. (It was then that the engine
Was sabotaged). In '39 for seven weeks
The inn was occupied by a punitive committee
With several inhabitants beaten up.
                              (And who can see
Or would believe that barren future which
Expropriating their own violences
Will put these enemies together
Under the coldest terror of all?)
                              Ilya returns ;
It is not only Stoyanka and Laforgue, but
Everything as well. Every world-view seems
To present him with horrifying contradictions
Or baffle his conscience with inhuman clarities :
He feels pitiable, yet better than last week
When he either drank himself senseless every day
Or meditated suicide.

                              II

Professor Mantev walks slowly every morning
Along the corduroy road and then by a pathway
Into a little copse on an island of high ground
And back in time for lunch. He is doing very little,
Occasionally annotating or correcting
A chapter in his book on Nogay place-names.
He reads the papers and is sometimes angry
At the government's clear treachery and meanness, but
He seldom really thinks of returning. He has lost ambition.
Perhaps he is getting old.
                              Two days ago
There was an accident in the lock, a man fell
Between a barge and the lock-side, was crushed to death,
Brown blood floating on the scummy water.
This happens occasionally.
                              Mantev was not really
Affected by it. In theory he is a humanist,
But in the marshes a curious lethargy of feeling
Has taken him. He looks at the landscape,
Affected rather oddly, feeling its horizons
As flat, receding agencies of life.
And the recession draws him on into a spirit's mere.

III

Maria Tomasinova sits in her father's inn,
On a wooden stool in front of the enormous stove
Which will not be lit till late October.
She thinks of Ilya and thinks it love.
And perhaps it is, or will be. In her heart
At any rate it moves more piercingly
Than many greater passions.
                          In this country
The primary education is extremely good,
And the peasants are politically informed
And read the national poets.
                          But still,
Ilya has the glamour of a higher culture
For a girl who has been through progymnasium. He is not
Particularly handsome, but has a distant look
And fading violence in his eyes and brow.
She is not thinking of the sexual act,
Which is uncommon in the countryside
Among the unmarried. But her body moves
In a fresher and more pleasing way.
                          The sun
Strikes through the open door and makes the dust
Into a fog of light. She sighs ;
And a light breeze ruffles the water of the marshes
And bends the high grass on the little islands
On which are browsing the small local cattle ;
Pirov is oiling the lock-machinery and whistling.
And far down the dusty road some carts are toiling
Towards Zopol, with fish.

IV

The Marshes have their own allure. The yielding air,
The cowmen's horns, the fish flashing,
And all the smoothness of the heavy summer
To some are more appealing than the snowbound peaks
Or the rolling garden country of the Central Province.
A grebe cries.

                              Yes, we all know
That history holds the Marshes in its iron grip
Like every other region, that next year will see
The alliance with Germany and the small beginnings
Of the partisan movement : in all the area
A few groups of half a dozen men
Occasionally shooting up a gendarmes' post
Or cutting the telegraph wires ; and a rule of torture
Set up against them. Pirov beaten to death
In the reception cell at Zopol jail ;
Ilya a conscript, invalided out
With an incurable leg ; Maria surviving ;
The short October fighting in the Marshes,
A threshing blindness of noise and lightning,
A smell of cordite mixing with the swamp smell,
And spreading areas of black upon the water ;
And then the coup d'état : everything different ;
Professor Mantev recalled to the capital
To take part in the government of the National Front,
And yet a more bitter cycle of betrayals . . .
And gradually all fading into their other lives,
With these Marshes and this summer forgotten.

— None of these threads work out.
We cannot pursue them down the twisting future
Nor form a close-knit tragic destiny,
Or even some fulfilment for the promised local lyrics
Of Ilya or Maria. No, it all dissolves.

Yet
Although this area has no especial beauty
And the season is pleasant but not unusual,
It is unique. These moments and these people
Meet in an absolutely new and unforgettable
Fusion. For this time and place
Like any other, every life must bear
Always its vague regrets, and sometimes piercingly
Pangs of nostalgia
For what can never be repeated in them.

from BETWEEN MARS AND VENUS

Art and Love

In a corner of the exhibition
He sees two pictures by his wife,
A portrait and a still life ;
Cyclamen bursts red from the pot
In a green material of leaf ;
And (hoping no one thinks this oaf
In ochre planes is him), he's caught
In affection and recognition.

But it is not anything in
Painting (or in poetry either)
Would keep them together.
— Not in a supposed completeness
Through the grand fusions of art
The deeper life is shared,
But by some fantasy of sweetness
And the honey smell of her skin.

For the 1956 Opposition of Mars

Red on the south horizon, brighter than
For fifteen years, the little planet glows,
And brightest yet its kindled themes impose
    On the imaginings of man.
War's omen once. Then source of fate's firm rays,
    Or, punched through the precarious sky,
    A hole on hell. And then a dry
Quantum of knowledge merely, cold in space.

Only in names from legend, history, dream,
The heart showed on its map the regions drawn :
The Horn of Ammon and the Bay of Dawn.
    Now, fantasy and knowledge gleam
One red ; and by the next close opposition
    Observers in the exosphere
    Should see it many times as clear,
And by the next one yet, match touch with vision,

Grasping whatever starts beneath those noons'
Blue-black intensities of sky ; on sand
Blood-orange where the blue-green lowlands end ;
    In thin air ; under two small moons ;
As spring's green flux pours down from where the pole is ;
    Till yellow clouds fade, while blue, higher,
    Catch the set sun with faintest fire
Over Arcadia or the Lacus Solis.

Pure joy of knowledge rides as high as art.
The whole heart cannot keep alive on either.
Wills as of Drake and Shakespeare strike together ;
    Cultures turn rotten when they part.
True frontiers march with those in the mind's eye :
    — The white sound rising now to fury
    In efflux from the hot venturi
As Earth's close down, gives us the endless sky.

Lake in Vermont

        After sunset, under the spread gleam
        And over turtle, bass and crawfish,
        The surface now is slate, yes,
        But also perspex, polythene :
        A disorientating light
        Spills out from that thick glaze,
        Concussively serene.

But as we turn, behind us
There is a holding of darkness ;
In the warm glooms of the pinewood
Already fireflies rouse
Silent points, small puffs of light,
Over the aromatic fallings,
Under the night-green boughs.

These are themselves, not images.
Yet such is the drift of life
That I cannot help seeing, saying
Other sparks now that ignite
In the warm glooms of my body ;
In the smooth grey of her eyes
Another indescribable light.

P y t h e a s

Heat falls away like water from the headland.
Evening enters Marseilles. And a ghost
Starts up before us from its rocky bed and,
Quite justifiably, begins to boast :

Outsailing, close-hauled to a Pillar's lee,
The swift black Punic galleys on patrol,
I felt her lift to a more living sea,
Her prow swing to the calculated Pole.

Cantion, Orcas — to fresh lands we steered.
Thulé was green beneath a circling sun.
Salt of a new sea glittered in my beard,
And still I turned her northward, let her run.

Till a thick silence, robbed of seas and skies,
Mixed to a single element of murk
The wet grey fog, the pulsing mush of ice.
— All this I mentioned in my published work.

Polybius, Strabo, scholars by the score
Praised my abstractions and astronomy,
But since it clashed with academic lore
They called all my experience a lie.

The beachside's dry luxuriance — cactus, coral —
Glimmers and he is gone. We sympathize,
Who see our literary students quarrel
With verse that ventures to survive the ice.

Love rots beneath that calm cerebral mere ;
Calling unknowable what is just unknown
They shrink the Ocean to a pure idea
And speak of Thulé as a frozen stone.

Galatea

What wind can cool the mirror
That weaves unending fire ?

Such labour and desire
Assemble from his life
Out of a mass of error
Verities that revive
In brief emotive gestures
Or hints of a physique,
Intent into the texture
And smoothness of the stone.
One night the work's complete.

The chisel drops. A candle
Assists the waning moon
To supernaturalize
The surfaces of art.
He can no longer handle
The pressures of a heart
Whose blind mythologies
Insatiably summon
Through to this further truth :
True, though transcendent, woman.

She stirs. And love runs free.
Yet, as a supple light
Moves on the moving curve
Of warm and stone-smooth thigh,
He still regards her with
The whole intent of art —

With passion and reserve.

Locality

Desert : to hundreds of suns
Acrid and sinister
In this bedraggled cadence
The empty hectares glow.
If filters the hoarse terrain
To kinaesthetic images.
And the lifeless strikes its blow
Again and again and again.

Sea scuffles its freight of corpses
Rowelled over blunt rocks,
And jetsam thumps the oil-drums
By the edge of the pebbles and piers.
Through curtains bulging tight
With glut of a queasy moon
It plucks at latent ears
Night after night after night.

Embedded in the city
As the last arcs sputter
And the sky is black and blank,
Only abstraction can face
The purged unsensuous flavour,
And venom and sloth ride high
Through an imageless, timeless place
For ever and ever and ever.

If You Must

Shut your eyes.

The great tides of the dark
Tug at your heart. Storm dies
As insensible currents sweep
Your elaborate senses back
Into the timeless deep.

And that is good. But when
The long waves cast you up
What reaches for the pen ?
A firm and honest hand ?
Or is the inordinate grip
Trembling still, half-stunned ?

Do you label it with
Symbols thawed from the cold
Storage of a myth ?
Or even, killed and caught,
Cram it through some old
Slicer of structured thought ?

Does the loud dithyramb
Or high dramatic pose
Overexpose the dumb
Moment of furthest night
When the great tide rose
And darkness subsumed light ?

Or can you set down clear
That sole experience
Strictly received, as near
As light can realize
To what flowed only once
When you shut your eyes ?

Great Lakes

As ever, the visual affect
Streams fresh from a new water,
A fresh light, different spectra
— In fact, from a negation.

Negation of sensuous habit
Extrapolating the blue
Sweep into arms of ocean,
Inventing the tart salt

Not only into the concept
But upon the actual air :
A saline tang or iodic
Effluvium of absent seaweed

Rise for a moment, ghosts,
As stiffened reflexes firing
In flashes of an old musketry
Dazzle the sensuous field.

Such shatterings build up the reason
That a new light more enlightens,
A new love more liberates,
But frees, illuminates what

But the riches of the already,
Stacked in sluggish columns :
The dusty, sleeping palace
Magnificent and wakeable

Which when the prince enters
Can no longer bear to be dead
But dancing, spins and glitters
Like these waves under my eye,

Bringing *all* to excitement
Like this water cooler than air,
A slight shock fresh to the wrist
As I dangle my arm from the jetty.

None of which must blur the intrinsic :
The green wave laps the beach,
The sharp air parts the persimmon.
They move or gleam in my life.

Karnobat

The black stump of a hill
Hangs over the dusty town.
And we sit in front of the inn
In the even morning light
Hearing the pattern of problems
Which everywhere nearly outpaces
The second wind of the will
Speak from these buildings, languages and faces.

In the golden face of this woman
Repeating the violence and pride
Of forgotten Avars or Huns ;
In the earthy face of a tinker
From the Omayyad hosts' disaster ;
And, as he jigs in the street,
In that errand-boy's Roman
Brow and his straight Varangian hair like wheat.

This is forgotten richness
That half of Europe's history
Strikes from a local dark,
But still in the open day
Turk and Gypsy and Greek
Though separately set down
Where files and feelings speak,
Share here the shape and squalor of the human town.

And can we share it too ?
By the stream at the edge of the town,
Dry except for the few
Brown fly-haunted pools
Of a buffalo-wallow, we stood
Last night with a bull-headed herdsman
And he seemed, relaxing his frown,
To seal with word and grin our common blood.

But under the Turkish tower
Where a sun of the palest brass
Gives violence to the dryness,
By the mottled plaster and wood
I examine the bites on my knees
Received in the sleepless hour
And to which in years I have never
Been able yet to adapt myself like these.

No doubt one would soon become
Used to the sour smells
That drift from the houses and streets ;
But here in a stronger form
The minor problem is set
That the humanist often meets,
Striking all poetry dumb :
To balance one's abstract love against the bed-bugs.

*Excerpt from a Report
to the Galactic Council*

. . . on the third planet too, life is found.

LXI

(These sections are presented in this form under the regulation
Which requires a local language and an attempt at least
To employ its fullest method : so that the Council's evaluation
Of the species may be in accord with the nature of the beast.)

The race is one of those which use (in this case orally) discrete
Invariant symbols, recombination of whose elements
Can in no sort of circumstances be complete
Or even sound as descriptions of real events.

The ' poem ' (at which this, in the biped dialect ' English, ' is an
          attempt)
Is an integration of symbols which may be defined
As a semantic compostion fusing what is thought and dreamt,
And working in senses and thalamus as well as what is called mind.

Moreover it liberates their symbolism from over-definition.
In that unwonted flexibility is released by the act
Of no longer holding the symbols' split for rigid fission
Nor the symbol itself as object, but as artefact.

Observation of real events includes the observer, ' heart ' and all ;
(The common measurable features are obtained by omitting this
          part.)
But there is also a common aspect in the emotional
Shared by other members of the species : this is conveyed by ' art. '

The poem combines all these, so that the whole scene
Can penetrate the biped's organism at every level.
With the aid of the empathy conditioner and the translation
          machine
We believe that the Council will find the method intelligible.

A futher note on this race is that, like those of Deneb III
Its reproductive method is the sexual, which has led
(Relevant at this point) to ability to conceive otherness, mystery,
Illumining life, thought, and especially poem, from the bed.

Before the body of the report it would be well to enter the caveat
That ' verse ' is better than the race's thought as a whole.
In general practice they reify abstractions ; at
The price of wars, etc., fail to keep symbols under control.

LXII

We can now proceed to the detailed evidence. An O.P.
Was established on the nearby satellite, from which
Descent was effected to the surface, in spite of the higher g ;
Normal secrecy precautions worked without a hitch.

Accompanying records show . . .

To Launch the Satellites

for B.I.S.

First it is fitting to name pioneers :
Tsiolkovski, Ganswindt, Goddard, Oberth, Esnaut-Pelterie.
Ley and other formed the VfR : whence in the war
Von Braun worked at Peenemunde, under the cold Baltic,
And the rockets fell, on Antwerp and London.

Peace turned some to vertical : they pointed at planets.
At White Sands and Woomera work went on.
Interplanetary and Rocket Societies
United the technicians and theoreticians :
And in their motives one of the integrities
Which are diffused in art, was sharpened to sheerness.

All of which leads to the time, not far from now,
When the frontier will be reopened, both to the farers
And, just as five hundred years ago,
In the mind too, on the fug of ideation.
Thenceforward not even the most hermetic in art
Will be able to ignore the situations of learning.

Under those unknown worlds, in believable Florida
Or deep in the larger landmass, intent on instruments,
This autumn are men assembled and urgent who have
Prepared a wave to break across the sky
And mount the natural cliff.

Non-Aristotelian Poem

On the second night of summer
Visual energies of the air and eye
Seized cypress, stream and moon ; and the tongue took
Perspective from a translator dream
Spread across the awakened, resting sky :
   This can hardly be put in a poem or a book.

  Yet I will remember
Heart, mind and senses finding one wisdom,
A single self not verbally divided
Nor rounded out rigid and wrong,
Remember the whole composition of freedom
   When the formal divisions subsided.

On the second night of summer
Time stammered to silence under a generalized sky
As that dream dissolved through the interface
Of wordless and verbal. And the trees flamed with art.
For thus through the frozen levels is thought made free,
   And the self arranged in the poem's grace.

Jet over the Pacific

The 707 fumes into the sky.

Ocean Beach, a last long
Smear of apparent white,
Melts in that broad flurry
Of darker land, which soon fades too,
The great artefact gaining height.

A view, then, only of ocean
From thirty thousand feet. — More
Distance, merely ? Larger amounts
Of the visual, to be filed
In dust, words ? No, for

— Even without, finally
The white mound of cloud
Heaped on Mauna Kea,
The scatter of swart green
Island focuses — amplitude,

The simple peal of depth,
Extends the apprehensible,
In no gross measurement
But the scope of the long light ;
Just because unusual

Only slightly, subtly, strikes
Undistracted out of this bare
Field of few properties :
Bluish, wind-blanched, a sea's surface
Through cubic miles of air ;

Extends the sensuous !
A not yet known mauve :
Accumulation of the slight stain
On extreme clarities of air
Hundreds of miles, to a roil of wave.

And the sensed is a deep chord
Of revelation (not grace-
notes on a main music — me !)
My neighbour, twelve hours from Sydney
Is bored. I am not bored.

And I shall not be bored by the view from space.

Small Hours

I

The warm dark room. High windows just imply
Two black, though less black, squares of clouded sky.

That too fades. In her arms the second time :
Pure night through which all constellations climb.

Abstraction at a pitch that's so intense
Black absolutes blaze clear to every sense.

The high elations shake him through and through.
And words break free, a sigh : ' I worship you. '

II

The rich ores of that barely conscious cry
Forge instantly, spear-sharp, to accuracy :

Not love, or not yet love, the sacred act
Speaks to that ' worship, ' passionate, exact.

The truly human action which of all
Seems most material, most animal,

This rite of adoration, thigh to thigh,
Creates the star-strewn goddess, the deep sky :

What all those churches shoddily declare
When theologians smoulder, mystics flare,

The long-limbed, clear-eyed Stranger, worshipped in
Incense of breath or transubstantial skin,

But for its softness marble, you'd suppose,
But for its whiteness, tissue of a rose :

For once those marvels flame mere pharos to
The unconsidered, absolutely true . . .

Through muffled glass, the not extraneous sky
Forms vaguely to his image-dazzled eye.

Sphere after sphere, the apprehensible
Shines light-years through her lips, or past the sill.

Harmonics of pure truth, slight noises spread
Around them, the soft breath, the rustling bed.

III

With gold so faint as almost to be grey
The windows hint of the impending day.

Passion of accuracy, yet no constraint,
As poetry sees it, makes the sage and saint.

What is the sex of meaning ? What delight
Labours to loose it from the brooding night ?

Here perhaps was accident, the Pythian voice
Drugged where the tripod's fumes blur chance with choice.

Futures may frame tough trainings, whole techniques
To make life language. Only poetry seeks

Meanwhile — as through jungles rank with myth
Intellect moves in speed and passion with

Pure instinct like a striking fer-de-lance —
The fluency and rigour of the dance.

Generalities

Late April. Taking stock
Of love, a long year's hoard :
What can define that luck ?
For love's a general word
Diluting brilliant essence
With seepage of other minds
And dead experience.
Who froze a fire that blinds ?

— In winter poems he tried
For strictness, for the rough
Undecorated ode ;
Now he'd be pleased enough
If sentiment were stated
Vaguely among these blooms
With his heart completed
And his words in his arms.

Baie des Anges

For once a simple image : moonlight on
A strip of gently moving water. Love
Makes it a system of comparison.
The clear unchanging tone and lustre of
This light is emblem for the purity
Of love's obsession. Its protean dance
From smooth and shifting facets of black sea
May represent the endless play of chance
Where the love's sameness never shows the same.
And several other forms will have occurred
For this clear twice-reflected stellar flame
To those who counterchange the world and word,
Whose senses rule their passion circumspectly.
But it is getting cold when all is said.
    So now let love speak more directly :
    — Come to bed.

Bari Harbour: Remembering Dreams

Light, light, light. The cool
And shallow day returns,
And into its refreshing pool
The heat drops like a hot coal
And quenches its night-won burns.

Yet in the shallow light
Now, a cold crumbling stone
And not as when it lit the night,
It seems it could never be lit ;
And I seem all the more alone.

— Out of this summer bay
Translucence laps the mole :
But who would welcome day
Unless made ductile by
Flame from that midnight pole ?

The Virtues of Poetry

I read in passing, or with killing thirst.
I take a draught of freedom or a sip.
The stiff dichotomies may slur and slip,
The faulty neural currents be reversed.

The tongue could be too salty or the tang :
It all dissolved beneath an actual sweetness.
Teaching no law and claiming no completeness,
It opened what we said to what we sang.

For it disbands all false habituation
That carves life up with language ; it will not
Disrupt one brilliance into *think* and *feel*.

Body-and mind's a fracture it can heal
In such a rush of luck and liberation
As grips a gambler when the dice are hot.

Horror Comic

Your bottoms are not purple.
But imagine a mandrill
Come like John Mandeville
To report on this people.

He finds despisal of fur,
Respect for the false,
Hate of fleas
And love of fire ;

While bishops bless
Wowsers, narks,
With snide remarks
In Sunday press.

But our mandrill marvel
Does not, like Lawrence,
Call customs tyrants
And draws no moral.

Is glad that some
Are made of wood,
Thinks ' dull the world
If all were same. '

And looking at mitre
And at blue pencil
Laughter shakes his tonsil
As at a theatre.

S u s q u e h a n n a

Two hundred miles up the Bay
Here and there high bluffs impose
Of a miocene blue clay,
Beyond which, flowing east and south,
Sight finds the smooth and luminous
Sedation of the great stream's mouth.

And over it from Havre de Grace
A long bridge crosses where the slow
Grey-surfaced waters spread and space ;
And the one tone of a locust-tree
Sways outlined for contrast to
The blurred greens of the various sea.

Humanity ? Yes : this white town,
Those fishing-boats' cinnamon sails,
And on that pale beach a brown
Girl lies and another runs,
Moving so that one's grip fails
On the poem's abstractions.

And history : the British burned
This place. Or upstream Ewell thrust
Furthest, before that war-tide turned.
And so on. Life, sea, past are met
In no famous brilliance — just
This ordinary conjunction. Yet,

To the accepting heart unique,
It burns to a breath-taking cry
This Maryland, this Chesapeake,
Breeding no easy lyric. — Come,
More passionate for accuracy,
And grip that vision, poem.

The Apples

Good and evil. And afterwards flame-edged steel.
But some mistake seems to have drifted in.
A belly-ache was brought on by that unripe meal
At first, but soon the imperatives wore thin.

Well, nothing could be done with the rotting core.
But zephyrs polished the other apple to gold ;
Then it fell by chance into sweeter mythical lore
And down the table, among the ambrosia, it rolled ;

And none of us have any cause to regret it.
For daring the disapproval of Zeus Almighty
There was a bitter competition to get it,
But Paris finally gave it to Aphrodite

Who ate it.

Vision

One sight I never happen to have seen
Is a naked girl by the sea's edge.
Photographs in a current magazine
Lead me to believe I've missed something.

In a field of corn, yes, and other places
— In the snow, half-naked on skis,
(Oh, very fine !) ; mostly with known faces,
And usually none the worse for that.

So if I do not mention Aphrodite
It is not for want of reverence.
Too formal, though. As one may find too flighty
All those cold-eyed nymphs of the sea.

Visual excitability, landscape, love,
Impose images : memory and myth
Will tend to coincide. Indulgence of
Mere whim, you think ? No, pass at life.

A conscious pose would not be quite the thing
(In spite of those professional layouts).
Luck, spontaneity, must work to bring
The extreme result. This summer, I hope :

On a clear day, a blue but cloud-flecked sky,
Water sparkling : hair in a light wind ;
Foam round her calves ; eyes, limbs livelily
Thronging the sublime heights of the mind.

E a s t e r n   S h o r e

The orchard oriole sings in the sweet-gum bough.

The whole Virginian Tidewater flamed high
With qualities and climates to endow
That efflorescence of integrity.
This ridge of sand and swamp still bears them now.

For where, in Accomac, wax-myrtles shade
White portico against the hot sun's harm,
Wealth, birth and power lose all doctrine's aid ;
The heart spells out tradition, kinship, charm.

The diaspora of that ancient race
Hear always in a commerce of confusion
Cities and standards of an alien face
Around them like articulate illusion,

Till, when they meet, they smell the Chesapeake
Breeze and see the humming-bird that sips
Magnolia bloom upon the ripened brick,
And the heart's language reaches for their lips.

The snapping-turtle drifts upon the swampland creek.

A Girl at Sea

Dawn on that classic sea. Pervasive light.
A timeless and translucent layer seems
To blend the surface into as smooth air.
Only the attention's far perimeter
Is touched by faint hulks of the Cyclades.

A sudden thrust of animal energies
Throws up beasts of legend and muscle :
Around the bow a school of porpoises
Cuts through the sheared and curving green
Against the turning moment of the wave.

I imagine her there, alone on the fresh deck,
As calm as these calm waters and as lively
And abandoned as those playful animals.

What stress of light, what trick of thought or passion
Can synchronize such images to one
Blaze of immanence round that yellow hair ?

A problem for the eye, the heart, the poem.

Evening on Lake Garda

The sun sets. The lake grows calm. The mountains fade
Into a darkness round the hamlet's lights,
A darkness welling out of the sky and the waters
         Until the world is full.
We can be calm now, but can we be more content
Than Catullus whose yacht sailed upon this cool
Water, than d'Annunzio whose rage was made

Brass at Gardone there, find further release
Than any poet who cooled his rages by
Apparently fruitful waters and calm nights ?
        Beyond that scattered shine
Of petals blown from a sea of starlight
Upon the lake, with accordions and wine
People are dancing through this dangerous peace.

And the water reflects the darkness like an art
As day and music fade into its glass.
But our poems hammer a no longer malleable time
        — Straining to keep our vision
Clear of a calm more bitter than those rages
They cry for unattainable indecision
As the ingot grows cold that took its heat from the heart.

A   Sort   of   Zeitgeist

Smothered in imaginary flowers, correctly dressed,
He skims near the pavement on patent leather.
The clocks are astounded to see him. They click their teeth.
And the Demiurge worries,

For it hoped, in a vague inertia, to keep the cosmos
Intact, more or less, from such deeds as of this heroic
Bespectacled apeman clutching a handful of something
Probably lethal.

Nevertheless the man in morning dress
With butterfly wings is much too quick on the uptake,
His casual glance out of some bitter depth
Of power destroys,

Bites like a cobra; till that entirely sensual
And blockhead Creator, drooling an insipid ether,
Turns purple and dies. And Shiva walks on and on
Down Coventry Street.

The Abolitionist

The clear-cut, alien fault he understood.
Thinking he saw a universe of good
    A fruit within his reach
    He grabbed, and made the breach.

Upon his rock of faith the Union broke.
Five hundred thousand dead repaired that stroke ;
    His own obsessions bore
    Into the risks of war

— War nearly lost at that, upon the free
Bayonets of Pickett's infantry,
    And almost worse when won
    Than if never begun.

For he brought on us, almost to this day,
The carpetbaggers and the K.K.K.,
    A running ulcer till
    Eased by a strong goodwill.

A sort of saint. And our own times can learn
How deadly such humanity will turn
    Which serves to decorate
    And justify that hate

Till it approve, in cattle-trucks and camps
Or under the interrogator's lamps,
    What treads its own first flower
    Into the filth of power.

Near the Death of Ovid

' Now life alone is left me, to maintain
The matter of, and means of feeling, pain '
        And the stylus loosed the last couplet
        Into his Letters from Pontus,

Whose luminous, mythological resource
For nine years now had held a single course :
        To work at Caesar for escape
        From those gale- and spear-swept frontiers.

And now, ill, he walked slowly to the general store.
Inside, amid the smell of rope and tar
        Among the candles and sour wine
        He talked to the half-Greek

Proprietor, while under moon-cooled skies
The marshes glittered with the hint of ice
        Out beyond the skin windows
        And the stockpot's reek.

And he thought, over his barely drinkable pint,
As the evening thumped with a Sarmatian chant,
        Once more of casual Rome and women
        And his senses' long distress.

He, first, had honoured Lucretius; he had portrayed,
Welcoming poets to the Shades, Catullus's shade.
        Was their passion for sex or reason a sharper
        Edge to the great gift? — Yes.

Watering Place

Through flowers fat after so much flattery
And pompous roses cured by tricky surgery
A rash on the garden's shoddy upholstery,

At the end of their six-hour parabola, the masters,
Careful as porcelain with consoling gestures
Return to nibble at their ancestors :

Fumbling with flesh beside the undrinkable ocean,
Drawing nourishment from the will's exhaustion,
The twin manna seeking under clouds of desolation,.

Now (as they say that some whose breath is needed,
Spinning downwater, from black ships unthreaded,
Fear more than drowning the cold slime of the seabed)

Worse than war's open furnace of the null,
More frightful than all bombings, they must feel
The sulphurous fires of an inner hell,

And caught at last by the nude accusing ache
Freeze in that moonlight where, a measured snake,
The tongue bleeds out its metaphors of heartbreak.

B a l c h i k

The sky is a pale water-blue
With the softest touch of gathering mist
    And ahead of us the road
    Twists and whitely climbs

Across the Deli Orman plateau,
A land of dry and fruitful stone,
    Across the former frontier
    And disputed territories.

Where writers find obsessive words
To construct a bitter symbolism,
    But we drive on down the gorge
    Into the little city ;

Buildings and trees, a calm sea-garden
Set in a crumbling dry whiteness
 Like a greenish jewel
 Between the cliffs and sea.

Cicadas enrich the evening now,
A caique loads at the little pier,
 Birds swim in the harbour,
 And the trees stir slightly ;

I find in this more depth and meaning
Than in symbols of the frontier ;
 And a sea-mist hides the town
 And flattens the clear water.

A Performance of 'Boris Godunov'

The fur-cloaked boyars plotting in the hall,
The heavy splendours of the palace room,
The monk intoning litanies from old
Parchment in the great cell's timeless gloom,
Keep tense beneath the Russian music's weight,
Demoniac or numinous with doom.

Even the False Demetrius is caught ;
The silver armour, dark-eyed paler face,
The Polish gardens and romantic love :
There is no weight or depth in all that grace.
Only the Jesuits are black and cold
— He knows them shallow, knows his doom and place.

Down in the church, vibrations scarcely heard
Beneath the senses tolls the slow, huge bell.
The silent, smoking candles give their gleam
To themes on which the holy paintings dwell
With artlessness that comes of certainty
— The terrifying crudities of Hell.

Even the drunken friars, the peasant dance,
The claimant's quick ambition, are a froth
On depths that pour into the dark Tsar's heart
Unlit by white Ionian or red Goth,
Where Athos, Sinai and the Thebaid
Glide darkly from Time's vaults, past secret Thoth.

But that dark river is the music now :
Not hope nor love nor thought can will it dry ;
The priests and boyars stand round like a wall,
And as the anthems sweep him off to die
The drowning Tsar hears dimly through their voice
The hallucination of eternity.

S p o t s y l v a n i a   C o u n t y

These green defiles through the green
    And tangled chaparral
In many fiercely run attacks
    Rang with the rebel yell,
Where Hill, where Longstreet got their wounds,
    Where Stonewall Jackson fell.

Detribalised intellectuals stand
    Bitter with fear of death ;
They hone to principle the edge
    That ripped out the rich depth ;
Offering countries to that knife
    Compounds their own thin breath.

Here, where the individual bud
    Blooms on the sassafras
Or bog-magnolia's special smells
    Rise from some small morass,
Men too made refutation of
    Pure system and pure mass.

Carpetbagger and scalawag
   Rule many old lands now.
Cultures stand gaunt against the sky
   Having no root or bough ;
And cold constructions of dead thought
   Rise from the heart's slough.

But here the Orange Plank Road runs
   Dark between close-set pines,
Or through scrub-oak and chinquapin
   Matted with trumpet-vines,
Cutting, yet fitting, natural growth,
   Accepts as it defines.

Rappahannock and Rapidan,
   The rivers of that war,
Wash the fierce brilliances to peace
   Through life and metaphor.
Red cedars lean across their flow ;
   Free people tread their shore.

Address to An Undergraduate Society

The Chairman forgets my name. I address them.
Half male, half female, one clergyman.
Few beards. The usual exhibitionist
In velvet or what-have-you appears to be absent.
Surely I'm talking down to these bright ones
Who must know at least as much as I do ?
But there are no incidents ; no complaints.
A nice girl asks one question about symbols.
A crew-cut politely doesn't share my views.
Why should he ? And what, anyhow,
Is all this about ? I form no impression.
— No, can't you see ? The poet isn't sensitive
To human beings. I see a woman as,
Forgive me, a woman ; a man as a voice
Expressing general ideas or limericks.

But fifty people have assembled (whether for
Disappointment or not is fairly irrelevant)
To look for something for which the young and poets
Alone retain their keenness. Something, comment
Or revelation, on the edge of that great light
Where joy and knowledge meet, ignite
And blazè so high that such tears start
As blur the vision of the heart.
Hunt through those tears into yet clearer sight :
Art in a crystal air, an essence of
(Let's not be too complicated) — love.

Keats in 1819

He does not yet conclude the psychic commerce :
The muscled mirror emptying the lyric
Or corporeal roses turned hysteric ;
Does not accept oblivion's lavish promise.

His body struck beneath concentric blows,
His love become a huge infernal fire,
With what strength does he call the mirror ' liar ' ?
With whose endurance crush the tempting rose ?

Dominion now they offer him to keep
Or sensual gardens, every summum bonum.
Yet — as such weakness never could expect —

O look, where in extremes for lack of sleep
The tough and bitter pride-of-intellect
Defends itself with vigour and with venom.

Kafka's 'The City'

They raised their city by the chosen site
In fierce dispute on how to build the Tower.
There was no haste : some future would choose right.
Once seized the idea could never lose its power.

Work waited on the discourse and the blow.
Add this : their sons no longer could believe in
The notion that a tower might reach heaven.
But all were too committed now to go.

And all the songs it brings to birth alive
Long for — through all those boredoms and alarms —
The fulfilment of the legend that foresees an

Hour when that city will be smashed by five
Blows of a giant fist. And for this reason
It bears a fist upon its coat-of-arms.

Spring on Puget Sound

So much water. So many cherry trees.
Both in blossom now ; spray under slight wind.

Above all, one of those nodes
Of life, unchosen occasions
When the extraneous overflows :
To acceptance, assurance, turning
Air calm, sunlight mild
On the poet from the interior
As the tensed journey unloads ;
And in the moment's stammer
No ghost brakes the machine
But a caught breath, as fresh wind blows.

Twists, ripples on all selves and surfaces
Swept by a smooth flow, refreshed, enlightened,

That phantasm is laid :
No need to define changes,
No place to be perplexed,
Seattle in a glimmering morning
Between fresh water and salt,
Between two snow-rimmed ranges
Olympic and Cascade,
Between winter and summer,
May also, perhaps, lie between
His last life and his next.

Man and Woman

Sober, he thinks of her ; so he gets drunk.
Drunk, he weeps for her. Drunker, he sleeps,
Waking in the small hours to absence.

The trees sway moodlessly to a blank wind ;
Right communication with symbol and sensation
Frays off hotly into silence.

Certain bacilli cause worse pain,
So do the instruments of secret police torments,
Yet here's the inexplicable quag

Into which all that towers fully founded,
Deepest assured, keels over fissured,
The universe torn up like a rag.

Other tensions rasp the brain and body
Rougher, stitch the tic on eyelid or in cheek :
Desperations of money, fears

Of torn flesh, of death. More real, you say ?
Yet those are not the things break bedrock, strike the springs'
Profundities : tears. Yes, why the tears ?

On the Middle Thames

To translate life, the workings of pure chance
Deploy consummate harmony for once :
With all components clear,
    Shine, flow, think, feel
    Assembled to a chord.
    First, air : those hours' ambience,
Bright on steep woods, the reach of stream, the weir,
    Raised to a higher power
    — Astonishing, unseasonable
Weather that has to sing
Chanced adagios of
Luck that a time of love
Should meet, should be, the exceptional
Days of a Berkshire spring.

Everything becomes landscape, becomes love.
Love flows . . . But watch the ponded drifts above
The weir that change as they slip
    Through sluice, down overflow.
    Not formless : annealed
    By the play of several forces
Ephemeral substance pours through steady shape.
    Squeezed to metal, shattered to spray,
    Chopped to breaking, thrown to surging,
Waters explicitly sing,
Not in bare metaphor
But belled beneath the weir
Where those whitely converging
Currents sweep and swing.

Bright differentiations ! Though they go
Spun back to gleaming unities of flow,
Always light meshes tense
    Stressing the frame of things
    As it too fragmentates
    In cruxes of devolution ;

Blues from high dust, blurs bright from leaves and skins,
   Fans rigour of the single radiance
   Till all the air's one transfinite :
For light may be said to sing,
Even in its most discrete
Reduction the photon strikes
Through what all grand mathematics
Pure to the senses bring.

And transitory. Another night is blest,
And it is morning. Pull the curtains. West
Swans float on flux and form enough
   Beyond our windows. But here
   More sensuous than all waters,
   More abundant than all radiance,
Everything, even landscape, becomes love.
   I need only burn in your breath
   To hear the great tune woken :
Love is a way to sing
Various yet unbroken
A cool flow, no less flame,
That bell-like fire, its chime
With which the world-weirs ring.

But can we find essential metaphor ?
We may go down to Marlow, in an hour
See the same water soar
   Another arc . . . Though analysis
   Be a high sweetness too,
   Why must such correspondences
Sound clearer yet what life is structured for ?
   Streaming symbol, sparkling cypher
   Stress more the pure original ?
– Life finds its way to sing
Beyond all self, all sense :
This mere experience,
This chime of the most real.
Thank you. Thank everything.

from ARIAS FROM A LOVE OPERA

Seal Rocks: San Francisco

Quite close to the abrupt city
Set on a circuit of bay,
Rocks shrug off the Pacific
A cable-length from the cliff :
Non-humans inhabit that spray.

Last night in a North Beach bar
I was shown, by a fine poet,
Arrangements of syllables
To the levity of dance
And the labour of thought.

Which it's tempting to match with
The accomplished arc, all
The swing of the seal's dive,
His romping swim in
A sun-and-spray sparkle.

How can a real being
Float, tamed to another's
Symbol, though ? The differences,
Escaping such aquaria,
Plunge superb. Yet reminders,

Connectives merely, may
Splash illlumination
Over his hot solids :
If his tight fury is absent
May spin the wake of his action

Across the more often forgotten :
Arrogance of pure art,
And gross humour of enjoyment
    The blue heave bans all dead
Choreographies, for a start .

Not trying to be, just being,
Subduing the willed ; the poem
Living the poet ; all that move
Amphibious, so emerging
Out of a dark, deep medium

Where they can live but not breathe.
Meanwhile, watching these
Big-eyed, unanxious sea-things,
We can enjoy the merely
Actual : a good thing for verse.

C h a t e a u b r i a n d ' s   G r a v e

The island holds into this big sea's surges
A nameless tomb to face the glorious rage :
But from that toil the image that emerges
Fades in the lost conventions of its age.

And when the tide goes down, and rock and sand
Join the high island to the trippers' beach
And melt those lonely grandeurs in the land,
The obvious comments snigger into speech.

— Silly or not, conventions cannot hide
The seas' huge swirl of glitter and of gloom,
Nor pour oblivion on the baffled pride
That thrust the memoirs from beyond this tomb.

M e a s u r e   o f   A l l   T h i n g s

Naked, she wants her shape
In index numbers ; starts to inflate
Her lungs. A harmless vanity. ' Don't cheat ! '
Her smile leans to his, a kiss. He takes the tape.
Bends, only slightly so far. Over the sweet
High rondures fits it firmly : 38.

Two handsbreaths further down,
Below faint white a streak
Still faintly brown,
A slight swell firmly
Presses his hand. He lays a cheek
Against it : love. He reads off : 23.

Then, holding it loosely with thumb
And finger, works it down, letting it slip
Out between them, until a sleek, hard maximum.
Breath shortens but richens, and perspective
Grows warm. Kneeling now he can look up
At differenced life. And down at : 35.

T h e n

Loudly the engines of the five Dakotas
Roared in a glittering glass air, ten thousand feet
Above the Macedonian rocks and rivers.
                                        Far below,
Minute among the clenched mountains a train
Pulled slowly down the Vardar's banks with field-guns
For the Germans round Strumitsa — no concern of ours.

— Now for an hour there was only a little danger,
A possibility of sudden Messerschmitts, but not enough
To build its alien life into our breath and brains
And sow the field of vision with its lethal salt.

                      No : that slight touch of fear
Was just enough to fill the glowing atmosphere
With extra strangeness and sweetness, and to help
The hypnotic engines and the natural brightness
To create in us a lucid organism
Watching the landscape and the future
Half-asleep in a mist and a dream.

                          And now
I seemed at last to fade into acceptance
Of the knowledge of death's usualness : that light
Seemed to transcend, purely, inhumanly,
The warmth and softness of a summer landscape
In which some dying rifleman might find
A desperate heaven.

                      The engines' note
Changed slightly as we wheeled to avoid
The guns of Veles. Level with us to the east
Loomed up the huge and snow-topped ridge of Rila.
The world re-entered time. I settled down to bridge the gap
Playing pontoon with a signal sergeant,
My heart still cool and new from the stripped vision.

                    And above the glowing rocks
The aircraft drove on, heading north.

The Return

He stood at last by the old barbed wire
And looked down the valley of mud and fire.

He thought of a girl and he thought of the war
But the past would no longer obey or adore.

Armistice day had come too late :
All he could do was sit and wait.

Perhaps time went on just the same
Until the demobbing order came.

The lorry rattled over the bumps
Past the graves and the wired-in dumps.

Back again in the old home town :
Some of the buildings had been bombed down.

' Darling, how your face looks strange. '
' A man may change. A man may change. '

' Darling, what's the bayonet for ? '
' All's fair in love and war. '

R e v u e   B a r   S t r i p

Nec fuerat nudas poena videre deas (Propertius)

Undepilated beauty stands.
The Texan by my side
Stops talking about cattle-brands.
He looks fit to be tied.

The feminine ! — He garnered it
From volume REF to SHU
Of the Encyclopaedia Brit-
annica (Plates II

to X, Article ' Sculpture ') — or,
Gazing at Russell Flints,
Found, anyhow, no Swedish shore,
No ' pornographic ' prints.

Those bronze nymphs in the entrance hall,
That oleo's pink shine,
He checked in passing, if at all,
On girls or eight or nine ;

So boys condense their sacred haze
— Not everywhere on Earth,
No doubt, yet where white statues blaze
From Athens to Fort Worth.

With wives and so forth, later on,
Life, as it often does,
Saw the sex tremble, fully known,
Behind that charming fuzz :

A warm, quotidian brilliance, yet
— As image — out of phase
With that first numen, deeply set,
That smoothly curving praise.

— But here the black wedge does not throw
A dislocating node :
And Iris or Aurora glow
As all his true girls glowed.

This is a temple. That last pose
Is Paphos. Less to love
Than make the incarnate circle close
Forms haunt the spotbeams' grove.

So the adored can blaze more free
And thus, intensely staged,
Focus in flesh its need to be
Protected and outraged ;

Where that dark glow between the thighs
At last is seen as not
Some later, special nymph's surprise
Praxiteles forgot.

Dictator

His head like a fist rooted in his abdomen ;
His lips like a leather loudspeaker, never kissed ;
Hatred simmering in his brain-pan ; fingers of mist
Touch the sight of that shifting eye. — A pen
Of mechanical lightning scrabbles a halo around
The muscle-bound solidity of this saint.
All the fluids of his body are irritant.
All its apertures emit prophetic sound.

Up on the balcony he clangs and glistens,
Freezing the worship at a pole of hate
To serve that blizzard's huge austerities.

But a warmer sound starts softly, crackle and fizz :
Fibres of fear that smoulder in his heart.
It is to this that everybody listens.

Art and Civilization

Where a safe hearth glows warm
The kitten show its claws
Bloody from some small mouse,
Smug to the shocked applause
Of the milk-providing house.
Outside roars the monstrous storm.

Deep in the wilderness
The huge beasts of the dark
Are killed with hard-won craft.
The loudest challengers
Rave down a panic track.
The hunter's tread is soft.

What blows the crude clubs deal,
(Swung with a discord of shrieks),
Bruise, numb, but cannot kill.
For only cool techniques
Can forge the blue-sheened steel
And train the sword-arm's skill.

The weapons that flash light
Glitter like swooping birds.
Blood rises to their touch ;
Yet they too but excite
The anger's screaming chords
And speed the talons' slash.

Shaking the earth in its rage
The monster roars through the glade ;
Coolness, to meet its charge,
Needs a strong weapon's aid ;
And clarity is but an edge
To the great weighted blade.

Reading Coleridge

Worse than to bear that albatross
    Humiliations have come
    Compromising my life
    In its search for a truth or a poem,
        As I think of the times that I have
Used prudent speech avoiding some
Material or social loss.

And when I find the excellent :
    As I look at the evening sky
    And the words in this book of verse
    I understand what they say
        Each in its special voice ;
' Repent ', all verities must cry,
' Although it is too late, repent. '

Budapest in 1945

Looking through dusk and a very light mist
Over the luminous grey Danube and the lamps beginning
From that hill of broken palaces the ruins
Assumed an ageless beauty, hiding the terribly
Slashed city, one of the very rawest

Zones in which Europe's hatred went
Absolutely to the bloody whirlpool's centre,
Struck a cold thunder over
Every usual noise and thought, and carved
Granite to a formless monument.

Gold light shivered warmly from the water though the vague
Evening. For even there, among all that
Debris of brick, flesh and steel, the eye selected
Blindly its focus. And so no verse can ever
Express the essence of the deadly plague.

Semantic

Dawn : a good wind blows from the sea ;
Noon : the shadow falls like lead ;
Evening : an amplitude of dying clouds.
The day takes form inside the poet's head.

Or he goes further : ' Dawn — the day's salt ' ; fact
Seems to dissolve into those tides of dream.
But (as, when concepts like *electron* seem
So sharp and are by that much inexact,

Strict wave-mechanics ripple to a blurred
Unfrozen matrix of activity)
He shows abstractions as not things but skills
And forms the stricter fields of subtlety
Around that simple particle, the word.

And reads dawn lifting from the shadowy hills.

Loss of Nerve

Once again the roaring voice
Builds its tensions to the brain.
Across the European plain
Iron shears the blooms of choice.

And soaked in tragedy too much
A milk of useless pity drips
Down upon the singing lips
Become too sensitive to touch,

As the European arts
Sense that we must once again
Drag back reluctantly to pain
The busy bruises on our hearts.

And arts and guns consider if
Our minds can bear the weight alone,
While the days like rotten stone
Crumble from the future's cliff.

Rio Negro

At Manaus the two rivers meet, and move
Their different-coloured waters on ahead,
Which, oddly apt as symbolising love,
Go side by side unmixed, though in one bed.

The context too : life in a lush resilience,
The damp green forest glittering in those heats,
Dazed with a myriad birds' and insects' brilliance,
Screaming with marmosets and parakeets.

Even the small piranhas, wild for blood,
Stripping the flesh from bone, may savour of
The hidden dangers borne along its flood
By all the witless savagery of love.

Finally mixed, they last well out to sea,
Then dissipate beyond the coastal shelf . . .
An image has its points, you may agree :
I hardly find them adequate myself.

M e m o i r s

In a square room he chattered with his staff
As reports came in to show his frightful error.
No longer could he work his well-known laugh,
But plucked his whiskers by the gilded mirror.
And, miles in front, men killed in fear or rage
Made individual tragedies that night
In scenes of horror Greekwise done off-stage
While his bright braid flickered in the limelight.

In some cathedral town his story closes
Arraigned more flatly as his blood grows colder ;
Ink supplements barbituritic doses
As, like their limbs, his brain begins to moulder ;
And history's dramatic intuition shows us
The strategist more tragic than the soldier.

Y o u   G e t   U s e d   t o   I t

The sensitive construct their screens of fantasy
And those who watch the world allow their hearts to harden,
    But there are always a few
The world's water always dripping on whose faces
Does not encase their eyes in globes of frozen stone ;
    They accept as true

The terrible imperfections of which worlds and selves are full
And the poet has merely to be one of them, with an odd gift
   But not better or worse ;
Unsimplified in the affective field
To feel the thousand radiations and vibrations
   And enter them as verse.

For the corrupt external triumphs and, in the heart,
The intolerable pressures of a racing engine
   Call for the ode
Of fascinating, purifying beauty which cannot
Be formed unless on waking every morning
   He swallows his toad.

Near Corinth

O nymphs representing ideas,
Come from that Platonic cave
Into a blue-washed air,
Or under the green of the sea
Lie in the lapping wave . . .

Believing them a false ideal image,
The poetic version of a metaphysic,
I yet think it would scarcely be more strange
To see them here beside me in the classic

Mediterranean light, real sea and place
With odour and sound (the citrus and cicada),
Than what we do so normally, but seems
No less unnatural as a view of matter :

The interpretation of her moving face,
Skin over bone and muscle, tinged with blood,
To intricacies of personality,
Pervasiveness or subtlety of mood . . .

O satyrs of a deeper cavern
On whom those sweet nymphs dote,
Say if such clear eyes can
Invent the mind of a man
Through the masks of a god and a goat . . .

George Orwell

Moral and mental glaciers melting slightly
Betray the influence of his warm intent.
Because he taught us what the actual meant
The vicious winter grips its prey less tightly.

Not all were grateful for his help, one finds,
For how they hated him, who huddled with
The comfort of a quick remedial myth
Against the cold world and their colder minds.

We die of words. For touchstones he restored
The real person, real event or thing ;
— And thus we see not war but suffering
As the conjunction to be most abhorred.

He shared with a great world, for greater ends,
That honesty, a curious cunning virtue
You share with just the few who don't desert you.
A dozen writers, half-a-dozen friends.

A moral genius. And truth-seeking brings
Sometimes a silliness we view askance,
Like Darwin playing his bassoon to plants ;
He too had lapses, but he claimed no wings.

While those who drown a truth's empiric part
In dithyramb or dogma turn frenetic ;
— Than whom no writer could be less poetic
He left this lesson for all verse, all art.

Far West

The tribes would follow the northward-trekking bison
Flat-forehead Mongols with sandstone axes.
Winter brought bitter war, ice on
The lakes, and the scalped bleeding skull.

For a drunken moment the routine relaxed
On a sniggering continent of goldrush and vendetta
Till Methodists with revolvers and directed will
Clamped down the railroad like a fetter.

Tone of Voice

Out of the raw materials of verse,
Great writers' words, all nature, reason, women,
The poem resolves into the superhuman
The pure description with the praise or curse.

But often now he finds proposed a smaller
Problem the summer's brilliance sets an art :
In their relation to the sensing heart
To state the elements of light and colour.

Once more the river with the sunlight on it,
Willows, the glowing air — a usual scene —
Draw all his mind and eyes, compelling to

Efforts to fuse into some lucid sonnet
Marvell's absorption into local green,
Mallarmé's cry for supernatural blue.

Houghton House

1

Behind the elms, sunlight on ripe grey stone,
The blue-green grass, the slow gold of the bracken,
A glow of ruined Jacobean fluting
Whose separate bricks have weathered into one.

The towers speak pride, intellect, devotion ;
The grass-floored hollow halls direct to peace :
The whole great building seems, in stone and space,
A huge machine to generate emotion.

But slow the emotions rise, and incomplete
Roused not by beauty set in stone or phrase
But by the watching ancestors who raise   .
The creative past, the centuries of weight

On the formulating centre of my brain,
— And then the patterns of responses die
Caught in that unpredictability
Only the verse can hold and perhaps explain.

2

It is seldom that all the conditions are present together
To harvest the heart. It is seldom that chance allows
Suitable landscape, physical well-being, weather.
    But here by the ancient house

Emotive bells of nature and mind are pealing
And I should be, and am not, in this summer prime,
Caught up in a resonance of air and feeling
    An assuaging single chime.

And the rolling turf and trees, a vigorous vista
Down to the slow sweet waters of fenland stream
Somehow today can do little more than foster
    An illusory tension of dream.

And at the carved lintel framed by this glowing view
I look half-expecting the fall of another stone
With a vague sense of fate, but of the ordinary too :
    As they might have done.

3

The emotions are truly there
But immobile, as it were.

No real tensions remain
From deeper thought or from pain :

So I take my pen and write
To focus its fading light

And the energies disperse
Through the loose dykes of a verse.

Film Revival: 'Tales of Hoffman'

Occasionally obsession
Comes to its flower, grip and shine
From the soundtrack and screen.

Light sheer to the glazed dark limbs and the smooth pool.

Integrities of the automatic voice.

Florid, impenetrable Venice.

In superfluity of magic a single note
Shatters the glass jewels. A dancer's arm
Makes a gesture that is love : and art.

Vassar

Petals on a fall wind, girls stream
Across the campus. — Now don't start thinking
Of ' petals ' as just a romantic
Property, the old dream-and-gleam
Of a delicate white or pink thing,
Choreographic, corybantic.

(Though there's that too : surely today
Censorious little shags might drop
Those screechings on How to Act Tough ?)
But the immediate image rings free
Already in a fuller peal
— Camelia ? Magnolia ? — anyway
Hard, white and smooth : fleshy ;
Veined with a spiced sap.
At the strained nodes of the real :
None the less subject to love.

Moby Dick

Ishmael. He had once had paradise
And now had loneliness. A shattering music.
Not like that albatross of Baudelaire
Or Yeats's swans, a manageable symbol,
But hidden, patient, huge and dangerous :
Heavy with storm up where the great waves rumble
Or , in black deeps, from silent pressure's load,
With death and terror for its metaphysic
That loneliness became one sort of God.

A S e a t t l e   P a r k l a n d

In Memory of Theodore Roethke

I

To light winds, tawny sun,
Recrossing ripples stress
The pool with arcs of dark
— Simple and intricate
As the opening oleander,
The opening heart, the run
Of tawny hair, light dress.

What words make movement tame ?
The bright elms hack down deep,
Roots racked through a rocked soil ;
That endlessly exploding
Sun blasts through the crackled
Corona's harshest flame ;
The glib aches in their grip :

' From the claws of a heart's crab
Loss tears the harmonies
Which make, which spring, which stun,
When the breadth of the breathed air
Freeze down to a clenched crystal
Pinching to one thin stab
Of twisted fire that sun . . . '

What says ? Here's true ! — This air,
Its warmth not wrenched beyond
To leave such shriek, such void.
That sun's a real all ;
And a right concentration
Still laps the forearm's sheer,
Still lights the grove, the pond.

The rock, the long sun fade.
All strength must sparkle there.
I find the light and sweet
A bough on a tough tree.
Her skirt moves in a mood.
Power ? A leaf that's swayed ;
A shake of tawny hair.

II

This sleek air sifts through green
Riffling lawn and leaf ;
Or rubs up the rough nap
Of disaligning hair ;
Or presses the green blouse
To scarcely need to mean
All nakedness beneath

— Though that's taut to transform
The day, tingling, young,
With extra wow, woosh, wahay
And sting of light, ache of
Something in the ribcage
That swarms and is warm
To what's so stressed, strung.

' Clawed iron of the burst
Bulkhead splits and rips
Where the drag of the drowned heart
Lugs up the cry of poem
That turns life inside out,
Cold tons sloshed through rust
On salt-peeled clammy lips . . . '

When's wreck ? Where's bitter reef ?
— Elms rinsed in a light haze,
The senses break with stress
And let me through to love.
I am wherever she is,
An image sprung to life
At the focus of green eyes.

Through blanks of scent and sound
Flame beats that pale sky off
The face that shows no mood,
The slightly parted lips :
Wildfire in the eyes
Looking beyond, beyond,
To love, to love, to love.

III

It hacked on through a rough
Year ; grace groped at fog ;
Love stepped in the town's slush.
The grey deposits of
Water, soot, sulphur,
Awkwardly wiped off
On air like an icy rag.

Momentum trundles love
Through years, lead in the scale,
Where under the weak violences
All horror boils around.
— Proportion, thighs and elms,
And all the delicate, tough
Clarities shall prevail.

And if the flame-front sweeps
That bellowing white-hot stain
Out from ground-zero's eye,
Or slit-eyed police-troops rave
More coldly through the streets,
The carbine in the ribs,
The arc-lamp in the brain,

If we fall, we fall,
But in the even-there
If live, live worse but with ;
In filth of doctrine, flame,
Bone-rot or broken bone,
Best if that swamp recall
Its springs : bed, torrent, air.

The green leaves feel her cheek.
Light, blood, are equal things.
We enter the great words.
I take her voice, her touch.
The world is as it is.
What sings could also shriek,
But just the same it sings.

The Hard Creator

He sees the forest in its iron aspect ;
Blossoms and boughs
Are tortured to extract their images.

The beaches open to the wind like petals,
He rubs them up rough :
A voice like, from those rocks, the sea-lions' bark.

Knives of nerves etch it on to his brain :
Building a life
To concrete, dropping like brick the song's shadow,

Laid out in streets rigid as where his city
Bubbles with bombs.
Wolves lope from a straddling darkness — that forest

Is set in a land that lacks its share of affect
And is not even
Peopled by philosophers and fauns.

Double Vision

The old mill's window streams with water
Blown from the mill-wheel by some freak of wind
Into a thin sheet down the pane.
Through it I watch the trees, the sunlit road.

A timelessness of vision alters
Its object for the art-imposing mind ;
And I see the landscape through its frame
In the light that laves the surface of a Claude.

The Mind's Emphasis

Illuminated in Time's shade
I see a gold insect
On a cat's or rabbit's shoulder-blade
White by a stream,
And in the water a rising pike
At the same instant :
A single brilliant memory like
The sharpened calm of a dream.

To place this isolated scene
I seem to remember
In Pembrokeshire, when aged thirteen,
By the Prescelly Hills
A glen in the tangible soft warmth
Of late September
— But the context vague, given its form
By a brain's effort of will.

There are other clear-cut memories
(Like that moonlit upper part
Of a girl's body) whose choosing is
Clear to the searching symbols ;
But to break the pure significance
Of this random shard
I grope for a selective impulse
Or separate aesthetic sense.

B y r o n ' s   S e x - L i f e

On the knife-edge between actual and potential
Mere heat of distillation may abstract
An interface where everything essential
Plunges the great dream in as great an act.
Once through, that act's a pallid image of
Its dream ; but here is art, perhaps, or love.

Where egoism and self-immolation,
At their extremest, border one full mood,
With almost equal warmth art scans a Station
Of the Cross or gawks at some Pandemian nude ;
Yet all that awe and impulse may collate
Only the windy half-world of self-hate.

Pulses of lightning blaze, or break, eclectic.
Love, only, lets totality prevail,
When appetites grow calm, affections hectic,
To eat and beat and worship and inhale :
Till art stands purged, to grasp with full intent
The disparate violence of that one assent.

Crude images of tenderness and power
Are rafts swept down a deep but childish tide :
The phallus, or the mind, ' thrusts up a tower ' ;
The ' wounds bleed dark ' in some obsession's side :
Hysteria may intrude its postured ' I, '
Or calculation squeeze all affect dry.

What toil can raise its constructs equal with
The status of emotion or event,
Not standing slobbered with a mist of myth
But clear and real, ablaze with measurement ?
For Sestos' ruins what Leander braves
A blue heave of unconsummated waves ?

Up through that imagery of turbulence
The thundered peak strikes grandly for the sun.
What most transcends phenomena, each sense
Most firmly grasps as pure phenomenon.
Strong words, and stronger passions, stand at length
Mastered and ordered by that greater strength . . .

Towards

The painter's pigments seem exactly matched ;
Precisely true the violins are strung ;
But verse comes from a more empiric tongue,
Ambiguous on the page its signs are scratched.

Its herbs composed to some correct infusion
The cauldron boils or the fire goes out
Unless a special discipline of doubt
Controls the winds of all the world's allusion.

For it is rich, too rich. It lays before us
Too lavish and too subtle images.
— How should such dazzled, fragmentary art

Halt its harmonics to a moment's chorus
Evoking none but natural purposes
Carved clear within the limits of a heart?

Thealogy

Homage to Robert Graves

God the Father, brooding like a hen,
Builds a good fug round chicken-livered men.

In what dry caves of Sinai, counting kine
Lean as themselves, a patriarchal line
Imposed their bearded mania on the sky ?
And what numb scholiasts would not let it die ?

Yet poets have kept from that crass emblem's grip
A sharper, wilder, bright relationship :
Cool, glittering body, endless as their cry,
Goddess the Mistress arcs across the sky.

High Ground

On love : how should the poem encompass passion,
Express love in some systematic fashion
Yet bearing through its verses the full glow
Of energies below the images
In that still unmoulded stream of molten gold ;
To clarify its purposes without
Their freezing in the analytic cold ;
To watch its many-levelled structure show
    The fullness and the drive of doubt?

Not merely aiding in a definition
Deeper than those semantics of confusion
Which mutter ' love ' until the meaning blurs,
Nor as mere celebration or mere comment,
The exaggeration of the passing gust,
Nor in the genial warmth or dazzling heat
Of love's invariable surrounding climate
— Of that delightful summer which is lust —
    Nor taking less than love complete.

Though it is true that some sort of fruition
May form a verse out of the partial passion,
(When loss adds adventitious energies,
The single incident bursts into flames,
Or single aspect holds the fading light
In the illustrative moment of a lyric
Complete among its flowers, stars and streams,
Or in some undeep generalised expression
      Out of the immature empiric) ;

In this analysis of adoration
She brings his search for good into completion
In intellect, integrity, desire :
Not merely fire and flower, the form of love.
(Though as I write my whole heart sees her blazing
Singly in a starless firmament.)
And then verse, sprung from all the meaning levels,
In turn helps integrate the heart, composing
      Its full perfection and assent.

Struck only from profundities of passion
It holds life's balance through that sane obsession,
Although the word reverts to its beginnings
When magic held the purposes of art
And naming cast the animistic spell ;
Till ' perfect ' seems the definition of
One woman ; ' warmth ' or ' fullness ' mean a heart ;
And ' desperate ' lives only in some adverb
      That qualifies a verb ' to love ' .

Existences: Zurich

Bad-tempered bastards ! — Black
Swans on the Limmat hiss,
Cobra-necked, to strike at
Pochards by the greening
Buttresses of the bridge.
Such sleek ferocity !
Imagery loses track.

For that shape is assigned,
Those symmetries on water,
To lace, marble, snow, breasts :
Squeezed out of it like milk
A metaphysic of white.
Whatever we think we think,
Whatever we mean by ' mind '

Machines, and those extreme
Machines the animals,
Engross in scoop or paw
The mere phenomena,
But we (where no autistic
Ideologies rave),
Seeing the jet plumes gleam

To rays of a G-type star
The colour of a black swan's eye,
Weave cocoons of echo
From the mist and shimmer of neurons
In their degree of freedom .
Irrelevance and essence
Trick out things-as-they-are.

Philosophies and odes
Flinch at these graceful demons,
Black on a shaken gleam
Where waters disperse the day . . .
Flinch and are firm again
As that western light weaves down
Through white-swan-coloured clouds.

S e v e n   A r i a s

1

As the images pull
The fog of distance apart,
Under that steep-browed
Cliff with the echoes calling
    I see the water's light-blue sweep.

The lake is clear and motionless,
In it in depth upon depth
Is reflected the changing cloud,
The swaying pines, the world.
    My heart is like the lake, full.

Throw in a stone, it drops
Through the reflected world,
Out of sight, still falling
To darkness, the water heart.
    My love is like the lake, deep.

2

Imagination is not strong enough ;
I see her dimly through a lifeless verse
Who glows in the reality of love ;
My vision holds her vague and motionless
Beneath refracting media of art,
Like that old legend's sleeping paradise ;
The sky and trees are still ; the hours pass ;
And only as the images depart
My love, a sharp jewel, cuts the glass,
My heart, a hot coal, melts the ice.

3

The barely visible mountains
  Raise and round their convolution
    Into a dimness of height
      Over whose snow the small winds flicker
    While the dawn collects its light.

This outlined white contains
  Shadows without continuation,
    A colourless sketch on space
      Giving form and beauty weaker
    Than can bear the mind's embrace.

But the faintest rose returns
  Upon one slope of cloud and ashen
    Edge of the far snow's rime.
      And though day floods in ever quicker
    That faint flame burns up Time.

4

O let the honey's odours overflow
Upon the gentle slopes of sleep,
And let the soft snow
Pile dreamily around, drift deep ;

And the ice-flame, the pure destructive flower,
Push up through the soft clay
As the sky's blue fires unceasing shower
A shadowless hypnosis, more searching than day.

Distant, a liquid silver, the eyes stare.
A spreading circle troubles the quiet stream.
Till dawn swells the cloud-sails, and a cold air
Cuts into the dream.

5

Once in a life the love that might
Strike out that whole life's chord
Plods him exhausted to its halt :
Dead brick and peeling board.

He sees the stinking bins, the blank
Wall of the cul-de-sac,
And with dry throat and blistered heel
Faces the long trudge back.

Love spits and claws inside him yet
While that numb toil begins,
As deathless as the alley cat
That slinks among the bins.

6

The waters curve before our eyes
  The blue brightness of a knife,
    A seed in a nightmare sleep
      To organise
    The individual life
    Towards a crystal
As clear as this lake and as deep.

Its frigid lens may concentrate
  All images under the sky
    That the eye or the heart can hold
      Focused to fate ;
    Soft cloud and swaying tree
    Enter the eternal
In a mineral, mountainous cold.

And though no images can freeze
  Into unwavering sculpture
    The living or even the dead,
      Such clarities
    Burn the heart and the moment pure
    As its mirrors make marble
What the rainbow bleeds, or has bled.

7

At least as high as any hurt
Numinous contentments blaze
Now as never, nights as days :
  ' Girl, ' as one might say, ' Art. '

Over all bedrock harmonies,
Under wide, cloud-rich skies of sex,
Divinity defines its shocks.
  Each seems to die, then dies.

COMING ACROSS

Some miles north-west of
Calm St. Augustine,
The old Spanish city
With its fort and verandas,
As we run by the broad, by the
Estuarine waters
Of the older Atlantic
Spread out in the St. John's,
We find ourselves launched upon
Interstate 10.

O Florida, Florida
(Floride incroyable
Was the comment of Rimbaud
Who'd never been near it),
White beaches, warm waters,
Pelicans skimming
Twenty yards out from
The white-fringed, the pine-duned
(The stone crab-producing
For that wonderful dinner)
Florida coastline,
We leave you, we leave you
As we swing to the westward
On Interstate 10.

On Interstate 10 !
— The continent-crosser,
The ocean-uniter,
Through the States and the time-zones,
The clenching of mountains,
The seething of rivers,
The glaring of deserts,
The rumbling of cities,
Westward, still westward
Into the sunset
On Interstate 10.

For days we'd been driving
From Washington southward
By Williamsburg, Norfolk,
To the Great Dismal Swamp, then
The sounds and the islands
Of North Carolina,
The strange little sea-towns,
Calabash, Southport,
The great famous cities,
Charleston, Savannah . . .
Thousands of miles to
The eastward lay Europe,
And thousands of miles
To the west California :
An unresolved balance
Between oldest and newest,
An edge of essentials,
As we just savoured bays of
The homey Atlantic.
— A bit indecisive,
Not quite committed
To the great looming landmass,
Looking backwards, like children,
Across the old Gulf Stream,
Till we turn from the past into
Interstate 10.

But now here's the driver,
A woman beside him,
A dog in the back-seat,
As they bowl through the noon-tide
In a happy hypnosis,
A prospect before them
-Rolling before them-
Of light, cow-cropped grassland,
Of pond-fringing woodland,
Odd lakes, farms and meadows,
That seems at the present
To go on for ever
On Interstate 10.

And now the Suwannee,
Dark trees, Spanish moss-hung
Over marshwaters moving
In swirls, whirls and downdrafts,
Upwellings and foldings,
Spreadings and suckings
Smooth as molasses
Around White Springs jetty,
But we must head on along
Interstate 10.

Hour after hour, then,
Girl and hound drowsing,
My eyes scarcely open,
Hour after hour through
The State's long panhandle
But we're not the purists
Who'd object to a detour
From Interstate 10.

-Through cattle-land, forest
Down to the Gulf coast,
The motel-rimmed beaches,
The sudden vast oil-rigs,
And by Apalchicola
We're in a new time-zone,
Then blank sands, bare pine-glades
Till we run out of gas, and
Find a motel, seven
Miles from nowhere . . .
Off at eight in the morning
Without any breakfast
Till in warm Pensacola
We get eggs, grits and bacon,
And are glad to be back upon
Interstate 10.

Very soon Alabama
For just a few hours now,
A low grassy plateau
Then, southwards and leftwards,
The greyly transparent
Light of the waters
Where Farragut shouted
' Damn the torpedoes ! '
Then we're heading south and
We're in Mississippi
And here the coast road runs
A mile or two southward
Of Interstate 10.

And we turn to the beaches,
The long-stretching beaches
Right under the townships,
Colleges, campsites,
An island chain southward
A pine-treed horizon,
And down little lanes
To Waveland and empty
Skies and dusked water
Until we turn back on to
Interstate 10.

Now Louisiana,
And we're soon in New Orleans
The node of the highways,
The crux of the rivers,
-Maitresse of all waters :
A hotel in the quarter
And dinner at Antoine's,
Bourbon Street jazz-dives
(Where Yellow Dog Blues is
Played just in honour
Of the visiting basset),
And coaches and flowers . . .
Will we ever get off along
Interstate 10?

Once more we turn southward
Through white Cajun townships
On long, still, dark bayous.
The Bayou Teche leads us
Under intricate live-oaks
And then we are back upon
Interstate 10.

Another dull stretch
And we're both almost dozing
And then we're in Texas
— Long days, nights in Texas —
Unintricate Texas,
Huge, glittering Houston,
Then the Alamo draws us,
Bowie and Crockett !
Names that in Europe
Ring as deeply in legend
(Well, almost as deeply)
As Ajax or Arthur,
And these not very ancient
Walls cast a shadow
Like Troy or Tintagel.
But we must fare westward
On Interstate 10.

On Interstate 10
— On Interstate 10 ! —
We drive through a rainstorm
The road swinging smoothly,
The two of us singing,
The basset-hound barking,
The hills turning purple
As we swing down the passes
To Ozona, Fort Stockton.
Absurdly pretentious
The merest of two-lanes
(Till we're west of the Pecos)
Now takes up the duties
Of Interstate 10.

Flat desert with distant
Reefs, rims of mountain
Like the crumbling walls of
Some ancient arena
From which huge spectators
Might gaze at the movements
Of coyote and cougar
Rattlesnake, scorpion
And men in their armour
Of automobile,
Caprices and Monarchs,
Furies and Mustangs,
On Interstate 10.

For hours before us,
They pass slowly round us,
But we finally reach them
And wind through the passes :
The Apache Mountains,
The Sierra Diablo
– Once more a new time-zone –
Then down to the banks of
The famed Rio Grande
A dubious ditch between
Parallel mudbanks ;
We cross a small bridge and
Drive to the huts of
A Mexican village
Crumbling, lightless,
Which might have been built as a
Flat demonstration
Of the opposite culture
To Interstate 10.

A contrast more violent
Than that between Juarez
And adjacent El Paso
When we see them next morning
– And that's saying something.
But it's hard to remember
As New Mexico takes us,
The tumbleweed rolling,
A roadrunner skimming ;

Up through the mountains
To the bright, hard-aligning
Continental divide, and then
Down the long canyons
Narrowly plunging
And soon Arizona
And in Cochise County
A ticket for speeding
On Interstate 10.

We drive on more slowly
On Interstate 10
Till, south of the highway,
The San Xavier Mission,
The towers of whiteness,
The vast baroque cavern,
The colours, the incense,
The columns, the icons,
For a few dozen converts
In mud-and-skin hamlets
Strung along the old trackways
Which long since preceded
Interstate 10.

A second reminder
— And far more impressive —
Of a consciousness different
From that which drove forward
The powerful conception
Of Interstate 10.

Different, impressive —
But in no way refuting
The opposite grandeur,
The endless achievement
Of the makers, the Marthas :
And only a clod would find
Merely material
The pure affirmation
Made manifest for us
As Interstate 10.

We drive through saguaros
Like an alien army
Frozen in stasis
Awaiting the order
To march upon Tucşon
— Ten, twenty, thirty
Feet of long rounded
Head, arms, and ready
To take on a tank corps . . .
But soon they give way to
Thin ocotillos
Equally alien,
Far less intelligent,
At least in appearance,
Four-headed, antenna-ed . . .
Forty miles from Phoenix
We come to a junction
And once more make an exit
From Interstate 10.

Long deserts, thin rivers,
Once more looming mountains
Grey-black at the skyline,
Yuma, and over
The dark Colorado
To the last of the time-zones
— California and miles and more
Miles of bare sandhills,
Then Imperial Valley
Once desert, now fruitfarms,
Then mountains like rubble,
Like a stone-quarry's dumpings,
Huge, barren boulders,
Pitted and ugly
As we wind ever upwards
And wish we were back upon
Interstate 10.

Then small Indian townships
And green Alpine meadows
A sweet air, a soft grass,
And then San Diego
And on to La Jolla,
The sea and the surfers.
And soon we are into
Los Angeles freeways,
Overhead and beneath us
Stems, columns of concrete,
A huge white acanthus
Taking root in the drylands,
And at intersections
Troughs, aqueducts swinging
A fluid of drivers ;
And just at the moment
We'd almost forgotten
Its very existence
We come to a knot in the
Midst of the city
And find ourselves back upon
Interstate 10.

For ten or twelve miles then
We head again westward
To the waiting Pacific,
Santa Monica's beaches
Broader, more golden
Than the Floridan edge
Of the almost forgotten
Ancient Atlantic . . .
But marking the finish
Of Interstate 10.

Right then, to the northward :
San Luis Obispo,
The Big Sur and Carmel
Till we're in San Francisco
— One cannot live always
On Interstate 10.

On our mudguards and hubcaps
The sand of the desert,
The grit of the canyons,
The mud of the bayous,
The salt of the ocean,
The dust of the meadows,
The ephemeral strata
Of Interstate 10.

Of Interstate 10
Which lies back behind us
Across a whole country,
A line on a map, a sharp
Brand on the landscape,
White cicatrice running
The length of its body,
A structure of reason,
A realised concept,
A white stamp of wanting,
A symbol of something . . .
Dawn shakes along it
As it leaves the cool beaches.
Noon beats on its centre
In the great stretching deserts.
Dusk strikes at its ending
Over Avalon eastwards.
And all of its lighting
And all of its distance,
Its curves and conditions
Accumulate into
Long weeks of image :
A section of life, yet
A respite from living.
So it's good to look back — and
Perhaps always will be —
When our single horizon
Our space-time, our world-line,
Our only perspective,
Our sole obligation,
Was journeying westward
On Interstate 10.

from THE ABOMINATION OF MOAB

Two Housman Torsos

Among the fragments discovered on the backs of the A. E. Housman manu-
scripts in the Library of Congress, there are two which have long seemed to
me to be fine and characteristic examples of his talent, only requiring a few
lines to be poems in their own right. I have here (in the passages in square
brackets) tried to provide material for making them available as poems. There
is no further pretension. The additions can perhaps be regarded like the plas-
ter of a restored statue : claiming no more than to recreate the proportions of
its original. I have naturally used John Sparrow's readings, rather than those
which have appeared in book form in the United States.

This reconstruction differs, in two minor changes suggested by Mr Sparrow,
from its text as it originally appeared in *The Times Literary Supplement*.

1

Stand back, you men and horses,
    You armies, turn and fly ;
You rivers, change your courses
    And climb the hills, or I
    Will know the reason why.

Die down, O tempests brewing,
    I will have heaven serene ;
Despair, O tides, of doing
    The mischief that you mean,
    For I will stand between.

Death, turn your dart and blunt it,
    Hell, take and break your bow :
[God's wrath, as I confront it,
    Shall fade, for He must know
    I will not have it so.]

2

Some air that swept the Arabian strand
   When the great gulf was calm,
Some wind that waved in morning land
   The plumage of the palm,

[Past Libya's red and Ocean's green
   Has sought our western glades,
To sigh the linden's leaves between
   And lips of Ludlow maids.

And lads, they know not why, turn south
   From toil with scythe or shears,
So soft it spills across the mouth,
   So faint about the ears,]

With odours from the groves of balm
   That far away it fanned;
And whispering of the plumy palm
   It moved in morning land.

High Definition

I hardly think that anyone
Denies the power of passion's sun.
From it all energies derive
And all that makes us look alive.
All bask beneath its potent blaze.
Some seek the essence of the rays.

And then it is disputes arise,
When, supplementing naked eyes,
Upon such heliac studies tense
The poets prepare their instruments :
Spectrometer and thermocouple
In skilled hands growing yet more supple,
Schmidts stretch out their resolving power,
Emulsions track the meson shower . . .

You'd think all would accept this rule :
The sun is hot, the lens is cool.
So, the corona's streamers pass
Unaltered through the object glass.
But there are some that think its heat
Their instruments should just repeat,
Until beneath a lens of jelly
The red sphere quivers like a belly,
Or, with burnt hands and shrill distress,
They cover up a molten mess.

Avoiding which, some hide the plate
Through all that sunshine, to await
The empty night and aim it far
Upon some distant, private star :
A useful exercise, its true,
But hardly what they're paid to do.
Besides, such life, in such cold hours,
Deletes the habit of their powers.

You need be no astronomer
To check which observations err.
Nor are theirs brighter now who think
To write in fluorescent ink,
Or match the randomness of flame
By letting symbols act the same.
— Whatever way they fake or fail
Their own skins gleam too red or pale.
The firm hand backed with lazy bronze
Best serves the image orthicons.
The warm heart and the colder eye
Best grasp the great gifts of the sky.
Poems, recomposing it to one,
Are yet themselves and not their sun.

Literature in Soho

Gamboge neon BOOKS AND MAGAZINES
   Is a convention which means
      You'd be lucky to find

Eliot here, or Waugh or Amis — Lawrence
   Yes, but as reassurance
      Only, a kind of a kind

Gesture to the bourgeois, the genteel
   Who otherwise might feel
      Ill at ease, out of sorts,

(As, looking at that pile, they would be if
   They noticed on top SIR CLIFF-
      ORD'S MISTRESS, which, of course,

Purports to tell the consequences of
   Chatterley's successful Voronoff
      Operation and Mellors' sad

Midnight accident with the man-trap),
   But we, under no such handicap,
      Are free to wish that we had

The eight guineas necessary to horn
   In on all that splendid porn-
      ography — beautifully

Hand-tooled, morocco-glittering books
   From the break-up, by their looks,
      Of Lord Houghton's library.

VENUS IN INDIA on the upper shelf !
   — The only work I've read myself
      In the genre from cover to cover, (oh

Surely you're not counting FANNY HILL ?) ;
   It s Victorian, formal :
      ' . . . *at once*, Captain Devereux ! '

An imperious girl completes instructions to
   The hero, whose substantive portion you
      Will have to take as read.

The whole book's very coarse and healthy fare,
   Unlike the COLLECTED WORKS, up there,
      Of (though I've only skimmed him) Sade.

' No expert, then ? Don't read it much, eh ? ' Yes,
   That's so, I'm sorry to confess.
      But if I did voraciously

Absorb it, some would call my standpoint biased.
   Either way, in fact, in my est-
      imation, they could speciously

Discover an ad hominem to pull :
   Arguing with a liberal
      Attitude is difficult.

But anyhow, wait till we reach the outer
   Salon. I know enough about a
      Nude photograph to make them belt

Up on that one. — Sade, then : a Bastille
   For a few years and you too might feel
      A little frantic. A Thousand

Nights, (was it ?), of raving lusts, on paper.
   Scholars find the dull old raper-
      dreamer most significant,

But *I* reflect, in life he gave some smacks
   To a girl's bottom, then dropped hot wax
      On it : dubious, no doubt,

But hardly, you'll admit, the very worst
   Type of sexual holocaust.
      Illustrated ? Well, don't pull it out,

For here, back from his phone call, Liberty's
   Agent — not one of your Garibaldis
      To look at, with those water-blue

Eyes and clipped moustache — in a polite way
   Leans through the sort of plywood guichet
      Blocking much of the view

Of the back-shelves. *Was it bondage, Sir ?* Well, as
   A matter of fact really I was
      Just browsing. And the answer's no.

Nor do I get much out of this rone-
   oed short story, THE HUMAN PONY,
      Nor RUBBER-GIRDLED FLO.

— I detest what these chaps read ; but I defend
   Their right to read it, and
      I won't think it does much in the

Way of harm till I see girls lassoed
   Out in the Charing Cross Road,
      What harm it does, moreover

Being negligible (in the very strictest
   Use of the word) against the best,
      Even, results of scotching :

Eunuchs, weasels, satyrs, zombies, goats
   In a frenzied scrabble for motes
      Might try some beam-watching.

So walk in, or (if a pony-fancier) ride.
   Meet, or beat, or be, your bride.
      Not your taste ? But, for example,

Who never wants to more or less tenderly rape
   A girl of the right sweetness and shape ?
      And that's a fairly simple

Case. ' The obscene does dirt on life ' . — Come off it !
   Remove that robe, damned minor prophet,
      And get something into your head,

Whether you're sticking solely to the Bible,
   Or are one of the new lot, liable
      To call LADY C sacred :

Life is not so feeble. It can take it.
　　It's also much more complicated
　　　　Than you seem to imagine :

Freud, in his ' A Child is Being Beaten '
　　Says the most fantasy-ridden
　　　　Most hate a cruel real scene :

While Himmler forced himself to be a brute. He
　　Relied on a sense of duty.
　　　　— In ' duty ' , power, even fame

(That first infirmity of nasty mind)
　　A mask quite like mankind
　　　　Conceals genetic shame

Which twisted, in some long-past generation,
　　To this unfavourable mutation
　　　　— Sub-men in other ways, but

As successfully parasitic on
　　The genuine social organon
　　　　As the tape-worm on the gut.

And let's recall how keen the Nazis were
　　On stamping out erotica
　　　　(Like the Stalinists still),

Which makes it all more than a little hard
　　To put the blame on poor old Sade
　　　　— Who thought no State should kill.

As for ' mere fantasy ' , well, would you feel
　　Better if it were proved real
　　　　— Or *became* most realistic art

But a bit belatedly, in retrospect
　　As it were, through the imitation act
　　　　Of nature (if you can call it that) ?

As I'll swear on affidavit, I myself
　　Was lectured, when eleven or twelve,
　　　　By one of those clerical beaks

Who, starting, ' Now, that part of you between
  Your legs — *you all know what I mean* ' ,
    While explaining how sex

Was sacred and swinish, branded self-abuse
  But had the decency to refuse
    The old terror ploy still

Practiced elsewhere, that it ' drove you mad '
  It's high time pornography had
    The same sort of acquittal.

No doubt you can get addicted to a book
  Just as you can (take a look
    At Hirschfeld there) to a fur,

A pair of shoes, a penknife or a bust
  Or even — a more recherché lust —
    To a nickel-plated boiler.

But even the boiler fan, (with his thousand-pound
  Fantasy to drag around
    In case he needed rapture,

Causing difficulties with hotels
  And a great deal else
    — You can recapture

The whole story somewhere in a back file
  Of the *News of the World*) . . . Meanwhile
    Even that, and even odder

Things appear a minor nuisance matched
  With the manias getting hatched
    In the mind of a do-gooder.

Mightn't truth be better, in a way,
  Than trying to make humans obey
    The various regulations

Laid down, it seems, for quite a different species ?
  Your little daughter ? One day she'll see she's
    Welted by your tight-boned notions,

So if you're laurelled with excessive guilt
  Keep it to yourself : once split
    Its juice is deadly, dripping

Like Upas. And who — if character defects
  Do cluster around sex —
    Shall 'scape (excuse it) whipping ?

Well, apropos, CRUEL NYMPH implies more action
  Than most of this. But for satisfaction
    The stuff's more promising

In the outer room. On which the complaint could be
  Not ' fantasy ' , but ' reality ' .
    But there's no pleasing

Some people. And, hell, what should I do ?
  I don't propose to visit a stew
    Just to point some apothegms.

For anyone with eyes in his head and sex
  Somewhere will like the effects
    Of the (still vicarious) harems

On the baize table — MODEL, TITTER, SPICK,
  (Though not the SEXOLOGIC-
    AL JOURNAL, thanks). Oblique

Sex stimuli ? Yes — except for beasts, or sailors
  Thronging down gangplanks of whalers
    Years in the Arctic, horned like

Narwhals ; (even the real stuff in Soho'll
  Seem pretty good if a blowhole
    Has been your biggest thrill long.)

— I've been waiting to get out here all the time :
  Less to talk about, more to chime
    In about with sigh, snort or song.

But look, what luck, the very SCANTIES 8
  That a bench had to reprobate
    Last year as ' absolute filth ' ,

As a result of which seethings the judicial id
   Fined the printer nine hundred quid !
      Oh dear it's dull, but a wealth

Of evidence against — not of course the printer :
   Just nudes and semi-nudes, not a hint, a
      Gesture obscene (if you'll

Pass a certain vulgarity of style),
   Depilated, no single vile
      View of the sexual

Parts — unless the justices now count
   These as starting above the Mount
      Of Venus. And there's FEMME,

Equally blasted, just as innocent. Well
   Instead of the fuss about DHL
      The intellectuals should, damn

It, have defended these good causes first
   — Excuse the moral outburst,
      But perhaps you too have felt

Righteous anger ? Well, let's calm our nerves
   With these unsinusoidal curves
      From which, as any gestalt

Psychologist would tell you . . . Better now
   Already ? I'll take TITTER. How
      Can we leave without a purchase ?

Three-and-six ? And anyhow the one
   On p. 27 seems to run
      Right through me. Phidias

Would have approved that as a major part
   In appreciating his art
      Even though wanting other

Components. Those who don't like icons of
   Women, for all their talk of ' love '
      Don't like women much either,

Relying for their sustenance instead
   Upon vague creatures in their head,
     Simpering, sopping wet.

I don't say, spend long hours in this mart.
   There's not much about Life and Art
     To learn here really. Yet

Unless that bit is adequately mastered
   You remain a contemptible bastard
     Like those censured above.

— Beyond word's fantasy, or vision's pose,
   Through sex and the feminine one knows
     Oneself. Then others. And then love.

Verse Translation

Sundance Mine Bar, Palo Alto

Tenebrous cave ! I chew my pen in
Undifferentiated half-light :
Right rendezvous to take to transit
Two tongues, two poetries, two cultures.

I search for word, for rhyme, for tempo.
The tiny, graceful student waitress
Soon understands I didn't *want* ice
In my faintly watered bourbon.

And that's Anglo-yankee contact !
Well, one does one's bloody best, man.
Hi there, Alex Solzhenitsyn !
— Bourbon ? Oh, I'll switch to vodka.

Far Out

Lessons of Science Fiction

The poet on Sol III
Too often makes free
Of a jitter of jargon
All structure far gone,
While around it the images
Like a cloud of dim midges
Or blatant blowflies
Imply that the oaf lies.

One might learn this sooner
By a look beyond lunar
Pressure-domes' cluster
Out to the vaster
Sphere of the possible
Where anything's real.

The senses ? Of course.
Take the simplest case :
' The grass grows red ' ,
Yes, he meant what he said,
Beaming it straight
From Deneb VIII.
While each colour and flow
Psychedelicists know
Mira Ceti projects
As ion effects,
Quotidian sights
Of those counterflared nights.
Then, the howl of Hine ' ice ' ,
The Arrakis spice . . .
(You don't know what drugs *are*
Till you've hit Barnard's Star :
Interstellar Narcotics
Says heroin's for hicks.)

Mood ? Touch of pure
Terror ? Well, sure,
— A psychotransducer.
D'you feel it too, Sir ?
Rigellian Thanatics
Go in for such tricks.
So give them a burst.
Sergeant ! Your turret first.

Words ? Any intense
Disjunction of sense
Is malfunction (routine)
Of the translation machine.
And that's with the simpler
Straight-concept transfer.
When it comes to amaths,
Time-twist telepaths
With *Gestalt* exchange
Beyond humanoid range,
Both species lock
In semantic shock
With half-crazed equipment ;
(As for what that last blip meant . . .)

Thus we hardly went all
The way with the mental :
It makes one too dizzy.
— But even the physi-
cal gets exorbitant :
Like a dinosaur-ant,
Like walking sequoias,
Thinking yachts (or destroyers),
Roughly humanoid entities
Who may have eight or ten titties,
And others like starfish,
And some polymorph-ish
By moments or eons,
And even Proteans
Who cause endless trouble
By becoming the double
Of Man at a whim,
Or half-you and half-him . . .

Well, all such perspectives
Are already correctives,
And we've not yet put forth
Those like nothing on earth :
Rulls (' Perfect Ones '),
Ingesters of Suns,
Equator-long worms,
Planetoderms,
Mind-mists on Pyria
Like clouds of bacteria,
Dimension-free Eich
And Riss and their like,
Thinking wave-patterns
(For example, on Saturn's
Ninth moon Iapetus),
And Energy-eaters
In crystalline strains,
And Sessile Brains
Sunk in fluorine baths,
And Ninety-G Laths
On a gas-giant planet
That twenty suns shine at . . .

And their arts. One note plays
Through thirty-five days
For the whole of the Horsehead
Nebula Gorsedd ;
While the Hectops who live
On Betelgeuse V
Take the Regular Solids
And launch them as bolides
In a dozen or more bits
To admire the orbits.

And their limits of culture
Might even insult your
Social capacity.
A pile of scrap a city
For motile shards ?
Suicidal amoeboids
Symbiotically bind
An android hive-mind ?

-- As for strange kicks,
All-species sex !
Tentacles, essences
Sting *your* six (or less) senses.

Enough ? Well, go back
By the spacewarper track ;
Take the images with you
Produced by the mytho-
poeic potential
Of the merely essential ;
And ask, back on Earth,
What are images worth ?

The extremes of verse ?
— Just what occurs
Somewhere, or might.
What's so thrilling to write
Is in principle normal.
What's not are the formal
Virtues of art.
Try *them* for a start.

Spectra

1

' SF's no good ' , they bellow till we're deaf.
' But this looks good. ' — ' Well then, it's not SF '

2

Space exploration is not yet emotionally permissible. . . . To find the advent of the space age premature, and therefore alien and repulsive, is the proper reaction of any sensitive man.

(An intellectual, writing in *Encounter*)

All systems Go ! The countdown starts !
A universe attracts our arts.
Three . . . Two . . . But stop ! He might get hurt
— That poor sod of an introvert.

3

These cardboard spacemen aren't enough,
Nor alien monsters, sketched in rough.
Character's the essential stuff.

The truest fiction of our age
Spreads subtler psyches on the page :
Half-witted pimp, blind coprophage.

4

. . . interest in science fiction . . . imaginative bankruptcy.
(an author-critic censuring C. S. Lewis, Angus Wilson, William Golding, etc.)

Imagination that debars
The deeps of time, the endless stars,
May grow too numb to harmonize
Its own rag-doll's two button-eyes.

Socialist Realism

Barren and burnished
The air clangs angry
Above the political city ;
Drums, statues :
The organization of
Absence of love.

Shops, full or empty,
Are owned by the queues.
The police belong
To the frogmarched suspect.
The censors serve
The poem's love.

Where the social words
Are gnawed like carrion
In a blank, blinding light,
Poetry dies or defies
With vision to prove,
People to love.

Prologue and Epilogue to a Limerick Sequence

Prologue

Our existence would be that much grimmer ex-
cept for the solace of limericks
  — A fact that's unknown
    To two lots alone :
The drearier dons and the dimmer hicks.

Epilogue

' Scorn not the sonnet, critic . . . '

Then scorn not the limerick either,
Though as Tennyson said, who knows why the
    Hell such a rhyme
    Makes the grim reaper Time
Such a markedly blither old scyther.

Poem   about   a   Poem   about   a   Poem

'. . . often writes not about life but poetry ' (a critic)

    To ride on horses (or eat buns)
      Is Life, and may be Song,
    (To sink drains, or interpret dreams,
    Or listen to a baby's screams,)
    But not to write a poem, it seems,
      That isn't Life, it's wrong.

    And yet — at least I thought so once,
      The time I wrote those lines —
    To ride a verse is quite a thing,
    (Sinking a rhyme, interpreting
    The wordless cry, the concept's ring,
      The field of sensuous signs.)

    But let the bays, the greys, the duns
      Go pounding round the course.
    Stallions may sometimes turn vicious,
    But art gets so damned meretricious,
    Horses are better than wishes :
      I wish I had a horse.

Visiting Poet

A letter to D. J. Enright from the University of Buffalo

Outside, scores of squirrels are scampering round the campus
　　As the leaves fall one by one, a smoky gold.
And between the Isotope Room and the Office of Religious Advisers
　　I talk of Modern Poetry and Creative Writing.
(For the moment this building copes with the overflow
　　Of several what might be called disciplines :
The atomic reactor is still rising by the football field ;
　　The churches exclude ; the Poetry Library is full.)
On the left, three types of Certainty ; on the right one agreed Hypothesis ;
　　With us, something less definite.
' Radioactivity : Keep Out ' is not matched by ' Modern Poetry : Come In ' ;
　　.It is right that they find their own way.
The promise of ' Consultation ' is too strong for Creative Writing ;
　　We simply say what we can : it may not be much.
I read a short story, leading up to reliance on God :
　　It is quite astoundingly bad.
A poem-shaped object is studied, all about fall-out :
　　The best you can give it is ' poor but honest ' .
The Isotope Room bears the three-pronged sign of atomic danger ;
　　The Advisers have a four-pronged cross and a six-pronged star.
But Poetry has no symbols. Creativity must shift for itself.
　　Come in !
　　　　　　　　　　　　　　　　　Well then, stay out, blast you !

from F O R A Y S

Casualty Ward

On a green plastic stool beside the bed
She sits chatting tensely, smiling
At the white face under the bandaged head.

Thin, not-quite-yellow colournesses twist
Down from the drip-feed bottle
Into his forearm, just above the wrist,

Cold tendons, or tentacles of some malign
Marine organism. And what lies below
The metal hoops tented with white linen ?

It was his strength she had most come to resent ;
His being, as it seemed to her,
So unshakeable, so non-dependent.

Yet when she's left him, after those five years
Together, of love then less, he was
(The first time that she'd seen him so) in tears.

He really needed her ! She really did fill
The role she'd now rejected as false.
Curiously enough, that made her harder still.

Sullenly, she turned back to rehearse
Old grievances : their row over that
Greek band ; the way he used to curse

At having to put up an aunt's friend's daughter ;
His shunning picnics. Indignation
Soon boiled as hot as ever, even hotter.

And strengthened so, she finally went,
The suitcase snapped to, the door slamed.
— And, in a month or so, the accident !

Surely in no way suicidal ? Still,
Some sort of desperate inattention ?
Or even a dull erosion of the will ?

And coming as it did so soon afterwards
What does it change ? Can it really begin
To stir the hard strata, bring to light old hoards

Of laughing golden masks, their Mycenean
Age of benignly beautiful
Heroes and daughters of goddesses ? A bed-pan

Is rushed to some curtained case at the other end
Of the long ward. Life and death
Keep their soft horrors. Her overloaded mind

Turns, unintentioned, to the fresh pile
Of problems in that supposedly freer
New life outside : job, shopping, flat. Meanwhile,

Though, to what high answer can she rise
As lips, once hers, now murmur numbly
' Don't hurt me. But don't help me with kind lies '

I Know not Where

Perhaps the best moment is when,
 His hand at the curve of her back,
 She comes in to their first kiss
 Like the bending of a bow.

— Near the height the old bowmen
 Would draw that fathom of yew
 Too, Lithe, hard, supple.
  Arching, giving . . . But no,

Wait a minute, how can
 That be right ? The string
 Is what the archer pulls
  Towards him, and the bow

Curves the wrong way. Reason,
   The organising hand, eye,
   Must delete the false start.
      — In another sense, though,

It's too late ! The greenwood in turn
   Generates woman : Marion.
   Then taut Athene, Penthesileia . . .
      Images run on, winds blow

On, blow on, blow on, green
   Leaves scatter till through stripped
   Dryad limbs sight bursts into
      Such stars ! The Pleiades, Virgo . . .

— In fact as a background scene
   The whole phenomenal
   Universe ! But at a strange
      Angle, by a strange glow,

Where even the flicker of an
   Imperfect imagery seems
   Itself a Light of the World
      — An arrow of getting to know.

Aurora: Gulf of St. Lawrence

Already the low shore, the
Outermost context, drowns ;
The sensuous receptors
Tune out locality, distance.
From the highest deck even the ship's
Blurred tons settle deeper in darkness.
Till there's only this flattened, stressed
Dome, with its writhings of white.
Merest phenomena :
A single mind and light.

Far from the screaming mirrors
(Sweats, secrets and pursuits
Where a sea licks the sand
And spits into the wind,
Or cadences tinkle and crash
At death or at citron hair . . .)
Simplicity burnt white
Is all that's here.
But who can ride the light ?

Not even colour. Form ?
No flame-fronds, no shatter-planes.
— Ions, simplest of particles,
Stream, white and silent
From a radiant in the zenith :
Bursts of non-human art, tight
In the lines of the magnetic
Field . . . What grasps the light ?

Knowledge ? But that's the self
Or one of its sharp moods. What
Point in the streaming sky
Can lock it into circuit ?
What long, intermitted, slight
Star, in a spray of lightning ?
What thread, what edge of light ?

From the dark behind the word then,
Cooler, extremer flame
Strikes through all senses and sentience
Till the great deeps focus right,
Matching the mind's tangles
To a rigour of the random light.

I m m o r t a l i t y ?

Cow Cow Blues — Bob Zurke at
The piano. I listen at first
— Abstracted, reading — with half an ear.

His solo starts. ' Communicate '
— Is that the word ? Anyway what's best
Defined as personal, near.

I might have heard him with
The Bobcats. Didn't. The grooves
Still catch him in the act.

' Dying amid the dark ' ? No myth
Arises. The sensuous moves.
The dead man comes exact.

Is it the ' natural noise of '
Good ? Solvent, anyhow,
Of the solids of gloom.

Nothing makes me think of love
Or virtue. Life ? Joy ? now
That's closer. I cross the room,

Turn up the volume slightly,
Close the windows and door,
And he's here. Here !

A simplish air, semi-boogie
Style. ' Died 1944 ' .
I'd lost the thread a year

Or two before. Even then
Used to prefer it slow, cool
Not so up-and-about . . .

Great things are done when men
And music meet — What a roll
Of echoes ! Tune them out.

For the great composer or
Writer wins us instead
When attention's complete.

— And it's precisely this more
Gradual, unpremeditated
Entry into his mind, his beat !

I flip the lever to ' Repeat ' .

To Be a Pilgrim

We got away — for just two nights.
She'd booked us in at some hotel
Over in the Isle of Wight's
Western corner. Friends spoke well

Of it. The name just slipped me by
And only half-way up the drive
A revelation came, a cry,
' Farringford — Tennyson's old dive ! '

Beautiful ! Unchanged in mood.
The swimming pool discreetly far.
The kitchens (for quite decent food)
Hidden by firs. Thank God, a bar.

Beneath the boughs, the green-gold leaves
Of this most grand of whatsit trees
He wrote — that is, if one believes
Old Robert Graves — of drunk Chinese.

And Garibaldi came ! — A plaque
Below a tall and swaying pine ;
(And in the modern Visitors' Book
Just you and me and Phil. E. Stein).

The track he pushed his wife up, on
The downs' low edge, to see the sea.
    Could a Swiss or Paraguayan
Dream of writing poetry ?

But now how piercingly my charmer
Yells ! Above her furious gasps
I hear among the furze the murmur
Of innumerable wasps.

' You see, there's been no winter snow.
We gets them thick in such a year ' .
Did *he* get stung much ? Well, if so,
His closet to the sure-thrust spear.

Our room. I gazed at sheaf and stack
While she's proceeding to anoint
The sting with sal ammoniac ;
' This really is a pleasant joint ! '

A notice opposite the bar :
The Tennyson and TV Room
— His cloak, his stick, some books. And — ah ! —
Grandstand bright through Gothic gloom.

Those books though — classic, pastoral —
That taught his verse its solemn stride.
My head still ringing with the call
Of Hesiod, we go outside.

  Hera ! Pylos' teeming great
Herds ! ' Unmoved the Jerseys munch.
' Koré ! Maiden ! If . . . ' Too late.
The old words fail. It's time for lunch.

And then, why don't we drive across
To seek through scents of salt and rose
The chine-hid church where Swinburne was
— Baptised ? buried ? — One of those.

On That Island

The etched Saronic's hardest blue
Lies back through miles of light.
The years' long lenses focus true
And on the heat-blanched height
The girl I see in the mind's eye
Trembles with actuality.

That lime-green thicket lifts again
Two pillars of bruised stone,
Black stubs of Aphrodite's fane,
Perspective of our own
Course through cracked arch, crushed architrave,
A sequence that includes the grave.

Intensities of light and love,
So urgent to revoke
The weed and thorn, the fading of
The white acanthus, choke
In that rank undergrowth, regret,
Clawed to life's stinging limits. — Yet

Goddess, or goddesses, you name
Them so to represent
The numen standing outside time ;
Pure vision, abstract scent
Sear off the patina of pain,
Strike flesh and marble white again.

In which continuum the girl
Who climbs the slate-pink stair,
The lemon-trees behind her, all
That sea-wind in her hair,
Purely immediate, yet shakes free
The blind blue of eternity.

The Poet's Morning

Bleary with bed, the bloody fool's
First act's to fall between two stools.

His breakfast next, as things conspire,
Drops between frying-pan and fire.

And then to work, his every squib dis-
gusting Scylla or Charybdis.

Far better if he'd stayed asleep,
Betwixt the devil and the deep.

Later

We asked him, did he really want her back.
This seemed to take him very much aback.
He spoke of her belled hair
Tawny against the hayfield,
Behind her voice the meadowlarks ;
How by dolmen and fir
— Druid white, dryad green —
She assembled the phenomena
And became their rune.

The incurvations of her breasts, her back !
That sweet beast, each contributing a back,
Played on the silken sward
Through those summer nights
Never quite sleeping
As hounds belled, hinds leapt
Through life-turfed, legend-treed
Glades, in that chiaroscuro
Of dream that is deed.

And so he'd felt it when they married, back
In '68 — a hunch he had to back
With all his life. A great chord
Held, right through the million
Words, the thousand kisses,
Intricate veining of
Happiness and unhappiness,
Ephemerals to dip, gleam,
Fireflies circling
A strength, a theme :

— The loyalties of love, when back to back
They stood against the world. ' Stabbed in the back ' ?
—He shrugged. At any rate
Cords of vision cut,
Ice-sharp, unexpected :
Collapse of green landscape
Under a doltish horror.
After the short shock
Stale erosions rotted
The sheared face of rock.

He knew the stream of time would not turn back
Where pike devour the teeming stickleback
In a white frenzy. Till even
The cruel clarities may
Grow gross, thick, (he made
A grimace) ; the sharp waters
Spill over sour roots,
Slump to oils of marsh,
Slow, confident rats.

And then, how had he tried to get her back ?
— The worst ways with a woman, falling back
On pleas, argument,
As the fire guttered
In wet infirm wood,
Tears, everything known
As useless (another shrug).
Why ? — A profounder skill
Herding the hurts' panic
To his real will ?

The load of loneliness upon his back !
Surely he did, would always, want her back ?
But the cramped myth, memory . . .
Green days in the high meadows,
Mists, twists of icy passes,
Now one far, glittering range ;
And in the foreground shown,
Galatea's opposite,
A girl turned to stone.

His lame conclusion, then : if she turned back
To what she was, of course he'd want her back.

Try Again

Things are terrible !
   Well, yes.
And the poem doesn't state
Or celebrate
Or give your own relation to
   The mess ?

But perhaps its job is just
   To hint.
You may think, son,
Those are cries of passion,
But they rather look to me
   Like print.

The Ruins of Carthage

Bou Kornine, the split hill,
Stands braced to the long frame
Of a parabolic bay,
And abstract ichors spill
From the bowl of a blue day
Into this bone-dry tomb.

A city dead in our minds,
Humps of disorganised wall,
Red striations of arch,
No livelier than the street-signs,
Place Hamilcar, Rue Baal :
The black butt of that torch.

No substance to its past :
Flickers of dead phosphorus
In delusion of deeps. Hanno,
A crucified sea-beast ;
Augustine's cauldron seethes ;
But the sharp umbra slams to.

Old images pulverised
By an inarticulate thunder :
To the blare of a blank sun
The desert numen burst,
And dry huts huddled under
The dust of Kairouan.

Night. No sound in the court
But the whine of the log fire,
No sight but the desert words
Clamped on a cut sky :
Algol, Achernar, Fomalhaut.
And beneath us, disorder of shards.

Like death itself. A black screen,
An impenetrability, rife
With brute abstraction. — Or else
Discarnate : she that is queen
Of Tunis, she that dwells
Ten leagues beyond man's life.

747 (London-Chicago)

After the horrors of Heathrow
A calmness settles in.
A window seat, an ambient glow,
A tonic-weakened gin.

The pale-grey wings, the pale-blue sky,
The tiny sun's sharp shine,
The engines' drone, or rather sigh ;
A single calm design.

Those great wings flex to altering air.
Ten thousand feet below
We watch the endless miles of glare,
Like slightly lumpy dough.

Below that white all's grey and grim,
The wrong side of the sky.
Reality's down in that dim
Old formicary ? Why ?

What though through years, the same old way,
That world spins on its hub ?
The mayfly's simple summer day
Beats lifetimes as a grub !

A geologic fault, this flight :
Those debts, that former wife,
Make some moraine down out of sight,
Old debris of a life.

(Only one figure, far and clear
Looks upward from that trough
A face still visible from here
— The girl who saw him off.)

The huge machine's apart, alone.
The yielding hours go by.
We form a culture of our own
Inhabiting the sky.

Too short ? Yet every art replies,
Preferring for its praise
To Egypt's smouldering centuries
The brief Athenian blaze . . .

That flame-point sun, a blue-set jewel,
Blazed blurredly as it went.
Our arguments run out of fuel.
We dip for our descent.

We drift down from pure white and blue
To what awaits us there
In customs shed and passport queue
— The horrors of O'Hare.

The Sacred Pool, Dzibilchaltun

The rhetoric of love : some little lake
Planed by the evening . . .
The image is a graft that doesn't take.

We slip into cool clarities, lie surfaced
Where, fifty metres down,
The bones lay late of virgins sacrificed

(Gold inlay long since broken through the slim
Wrists) to the Rain God.
It's raining now. Poor context for a swim.

Sundowner

Gin and not much tonic is among
The moment's contents, certainly ;
Also the implied relaxation
Specially welcome after his long

Trouble. But the sunset's passed
And it's that English indeterminate
Half-light, quarter-light. On the balcony
He sits, sips, sips again, his eyes fast

On high trees that edge the park, curving away
West, dark-muffled but still sensed
As green ; engrailed, incredibly intricate,
Yet a long running unity against the stray

Faintly luminous sky — itself no
Monochrome, but just moisture-mottled
To hardly perceptible shifts of shade :
Smoke-blues and darker. The senses' slow

Recovery ! Though all was abstract, yet
His body had felt lately as though
Suffering one great internal bruise.
Smoke from his Schimmelpenninck Duet

Spills upwards, spreading, to much the same
Grey-blue, then blue-grey, as the high sky.
From the open window a buzz-mute trumpet
Riffs softly affirmative. On his bare forearm,

Hard to say whether warming or cooling
It, a slightest movement of air burrs.
In fine, all the sensuous — unstressed,
Unhurried — is a calm tide piling

Up slowly in a closed cove. And as (back
Behind the still sharpening silhouette
Of fretted foliage) that peaceable
Sky, though nòt yet a blind black,

Turns now the opposite of iridescent,
Absorbing, not emitting, light,
He doesn't feel like a ruined man.
So perhaps he isn't.

The Phases of Venus

Defences a weak man may set
Against reality include
Ability to quite forget
A lost love in the nude.

A scorched earth policy ? — you're wrong.
Not fire but salt : a waste terrain
Scarred sterile by such frantic prongs
That no seed sprouts again.

Yet, till that peach-gold truly blurs,
The marble index of a mind
May file such fruit, till it recurs,
In a hard Paphian rind.

Too far abstracted, stone to star,
Mere white transcendence eased our eyes ;
Till now, hot poisoned pressures char
That last love from the skies.

Appalachian Convalescence

Eastward, etched in purple by a sun
Invisible behind us, the Great Smokies
Loom clear through a transcendent unconcern.

In this valley nothing strong, no love,
No despair, no stabbing memory even,
Has had me. And yet, such a negative

Is false as saying that we do not see
The almost fallen sun behind this hillside
While we stare east through its fecundity.

All passion spent ? No passions even start.
Yet here tranquility's an active radiance,
The slow pulse strong from the unbroken heart.

So fade along the westering Tennessee
Light of all conscious feeling ! Let the night-time
Confirm, as once it clawed, a mind made free.

In No Time

   Wednesday July the 26th
Nineteen seventy-two,
Which mayn't mean much to you,
Was — at least on a Buddhist view —
   My dearest, deepest day.

   Nothing whatever happened.
I didn't even breathe
— Literally ! The whole seethe
Of love, hate, thought, faith
   In world or woman wasn't.

   We flew at mid-Pacific
In a flick — not even that :
No skip of the heartbeat
Or drop of the jet's note —
   From 25th to 27th.

   M 31 in Andromeda,
Northward blur of light
— The limit of naked sight —
Declared distance right :
   But duration's by days !

   Metaphysic ? conceit ?
Then why the odd feeling
Of the missed, conceived thing,
An absurd soft sting ?
   Ten thousand metres below

The International Date Line
Lay, abstract, upon a smooth-
looking, starlit wraith
Of a sea. Faintest froth
    Outlined unnaturally

Regular walls — artefact
Of polyps, not thought,
Each, though, a seeming fort
Strung silent in support
    On the Tongan approaches . . .

Well, what (which I've not done)
Of those who gain a day
Going the other way
With the same date twice ? Do they,
    Would I, come to that,

' Have my time over again '
At least that once ? Correct
Retrieved regret, perfect
A little some lapsed act
    Of Nandi or Suva

In Papeete ? But that's a mere
Thought and I yet feel
As in a crazed way real
My lost unwasted shell
    With whorls of nothing.

Days after one in the Nineteen-
blanks (or Twenty-blanks if I last
A little longer than most)
Will have the same taste
    Perhaps : sweet or insipid ?

What coronals of answers ! . . .
As for that Wednesday the rest
Of you had but I missed
— Was mine really the best ?
    We arrive at ourselves.

Get Lost, Gulag Archipelago!

' The present Soviet generation is not obsessed with
the errors of the past. It looks to the future . . . '

For years those dreary old complaints
That we'd unfairly snuffed the lives
(We've never claimed we're plaster saints)
Of husbands, brothers, sisters, wives.

Thank God for the present lot !
They won't act up like those others.
After all, we only shot
Their fathers, uncles, aunts and mothers.

Then and There

When every block of every street
In Soho served one as a beat
Most tarts were awful. Still, there were
A nereid up on Soho Square,
An empress by the Caves de France . . .
But she who really took one's glance
Moved in the semblance of a bride
Along the sunlit stretch outside
That restaurant opposite St Anne's
(As if that's where they'd called her banns).
Not overplayed — just lacy-bodiced,
Wisp-veiled, white-nosegayed, modest . . .
     It's many years now since the nation's
Elected banned such decorations
To London — used their solemn powers
To screen from sight those fragile flowers.
High windows now may blur a face,
Illuminated bell-pushes
With ' Marianne ' ' Marlene ' and ' Merle '
Obliquely offer some strange girl ;

Advertisements pinned up, past counting,
' Beautiful butterfly : needs mounting, '
' Wendy welcomes old and new
Friends at No. 32, '
' Model, ' ' Governess, ' ' Masseuse ' . . .
Such verbal emblems fade, while hers
Unspoken, rosy, pale — the Spring's
Bright sign — endures.
                              Her image rings
With greater certainty of tone
Than girls' I've actually known,
Whose well-grasped lineaments disperse
Into that misty universe
Where memory, conception, form
Swirl thickly in too blurred a swarm.

      Recalled not even once a year
Why does her image curve so clear ?
I never spoke to her, let alone
Went further. In fact, what ' went on '
In this subliminal transmission
For me was vision, only vision.
What does it mean ? I hardly know.
I think it rather goes to show.

A Visit to the Evans Country

(Rondeau for K. A.)

' Just one sip, ' cooed Evans. What he'd spent on
A bottle of crème-de-menthe at The Old Ship
Was worth it perhaps ? ' How old are you ?, ' he went on.
' Sixteen. ' Thank Christ, this time no risk of Penton-
ville (an anxious point to bastards bent on
The work of Dai). Gwen let the green dew slip
Over the red rose of her lower lip,
And Evans buzzed in like a bee intent on
      Just one sip.

' No, that's your fourth, not fifth. ' Her left breast leant on
His shoulder as he moved to shift his grip.
' It's dark now. ' The sky gleamed, a pewter tent on
Rhydd beach . . . But, Christ, he'd laid the sentiment on
Sufficient so it wouldn't sound too flip :
      ' Just unzip. '

Heraldry

for A. P.

Alone, or at any rate cornered in his heart
Like most of us, by a hot breath of error,
He pushes roots into a nourishing past
To find in depths of that receding mirror
What cannot fade or tremble
A symbol
Like some rare moment of unbitter art.

For he takes talisman against the storms
Not from the total history's stinking press ;
But phrased in long-forgotten vanity
The timeless motto or, tricked in clear MS,
Quarterly argent and sable
A label
Gules : which are certainties, platonic Forms,

In what way differing from theirs who will
Hatchment of theory on the centuries,
Breeding not harmless talbot, wyvern, but
Beasts of abstraction ? — From a field that lies
Goutté de sang in real
Blood, not enamel,
Hobbyists of dogma turn on us, and kill.

After Writing an Obituary

Of course he's here. It's just his sort of party.
I think I hear him in the other room.
I'll wait until I've crawled clear of his doom.

Paralysed by a spider, wrapped in web-silk
Spun to contain the stung, the nearly dead,
His life seems just some clenching in my head,

A closed compaction to the sort of essay
About the famous dead one had to write
When one was still an undergraduate

— In his case well deserved: the poise, the spacing.
Fame now ? Mine were no more than instant glyphs
Of death-called lightning, not the deep-carved cliffs

With their inscriptions rich in fuller praises
From integrating centuries — and yet in a
Fulgurous flash one stamps the retina !

' To no one shall we sell, deny ' — so Magna
Carta runs : and then it adds ' *delay* —
Justice. ' Must he, beyond his dying day

Find court after court, appeal after appeal ?
Each century may overturn the rest.
— To hell with them ! My verdict stands as best.

Another, older friend, (of cooler talent),
Once told me that he didn't in the least
Mind dying. Even lives that missed their feast

— Made do on skimpy rations of work, women,
Laughter, travel, suffering, drink — unload
In a half-reluctant ' one more for the road . . . '

With him ? One hardly knows. His writings conjure
Old melancholies, shaded to acceptance
With such a power as may refute their sense.

To grasp him fully ? We commune in demotic.
After such flickering talk I have to try
To find the idiom of eternity.

He walks toward us with a mug of Irish.
A dead man walking ? Well, but aren't we all ?
My typewriter's not killed him past recall.

' — I never read such balls as Balbus' latest.
I'm a bit pissed . . . Christ, look ! Those tits, that bum ! '
— The nail of some colossal statue's thumb ?

1944 and After

Pinned down in the little valley — in its way
A trap, or would be if they had the strength.
Not very dangerous, with a little care.
Still, a long day
Pressed into hollows in the rocky, bare
Untrenchable soil, without food or drink
Or anything much to think
About , damp, coldish, shiny air . . .
Until, near dusk, at length
A few guns, manhandled across the bridgeless
Black ravine, suppress
The enemy strong-points, in a thundering glare.

Later, lost love pinned him down for years
But the relief came up at last — again
Covered the breakthrough to the warm, wide plain.

Life itself, some say, is just such waiting
Hemmed in a closed cirque of one's own creating
As cramped decade after decade runs
Towards the dusk. — But where are the guns ?

Two at Lake Tenaya

Not far below the ten thousand foot
Tioga Pass — the Sierra's highest — on rock
And lake the light lies delicate.

Under intricacy of pine-needles and
· Simplicity of darkening green shadow
We come out on to the white sand,

See grey-white of that planed rock-face
Slip without stress into the concentrated
Blue flame of the fluent surface,

Under pale, infinitely recessive
Blues of the sky. Fine air lets clarity
Range free, far. And yet if

You inhale pure oxygen
Colours around you brighten instantly, so
Shouldn't the lack of it deaden ?

But the faintest shadings come through
More accurate here, no less subtle, (white
In everything, even that full blue).

Like the old ascetics, we gain
Attenuation's own intensity — rich
Vision in the scanted brain.

She's naturally the focus. Her eyes
So matching the lake's hot blue, contrasting so
With the faint blue of the skies.

But more — behind clear gaze, firm bone,
Fresh candours hold that serious face serene
In the light's trueness of tone.

So if you've brought love to the High
Sierra, don't let it sink to scenes below
The edge of the sky, the edge of the eye,

As you ride down from Lake Tenaya
Quickened beyond image, yet forever infused in
A white bowl half-filled with blue fire.

THE EYE OF THE STORM

Halemaumau Firepit

We scramble down sliding ashes
To a Lost World sunk under high grey-black
Bluffs : Kilauea caldera's hot
Mile on mile of lump-lava, scab-rock,
Satin-black or cinder-black
Around green sulphur-patches ;
Sharp crumblings underfoot,
Sulphurous, silicate.
We cough, in the grey light,
At jetting steam, sputtering smoke,
Puffs like spurting matches.

Till we reach, by its Western side,
This broad near-circle, clear-cut,
And gaze down thousand foot
Blacker cliffs, at the slow writhe
Of fire-fluid. Red, red, red,
With blackness just turning to red,
Solids just starting to seethe :
A hump in the huge world-magma mass
Here breaking the surface, blood through skin.

We stand closer, her hand in mine.

The faint love-glow lapping the two of us
May not seem to compete
With the gross heat from the world's gut.
— How thin the crust over raving
Miles of flame ! And yet this mere film
Of solid has saved, is saving . . .

We still stand in the high realm.

And what's between us and that which opens
Everywhere, daily : the firepit
Of lies and terror — the flame-weapons,
The blood-ideologies ? What but·
Those small defences she and I
— Like others — may yet prove enough :
Love and sanity,
Sanity and love.

Porlock: One in Four

Going up the hill in bottom gear
The engine labours, a rising scream,
Growing insupportable, like fear

Blind, staggering at an extreme
Cliff-edge of subhuman singing

So strange at last is this
Clatter of levers bringing
Easier breathing, loosened emphasis.

High

The sun cried in the air, bleeding and blonde,
Its heavy assurances of eclipse.
But still the Sybil did not move her lips.
We felt the mountains ravening around
Us, occasion viciously sought
For avalanche. Far from the valley's fond
Babel of purple insolence we found
Astringent, unifying ways of thought.

We crossed the pass before the mad girl spoke
— An incomprehensible tentacle of speech,
A murmur from heart's mind and furtive convulsions,
Charring image to ash in the iris of each
Of us. Ice clamped the pools. The clouds awoke.
And the answering current flickered in our brains.

Here's How

From a passenger chopper on
The Santa Catalina run
Suddenly the Englishman

Sees, far below, the *Queen
Mary*, celled in her own
Closed concrete lagoon.

Was it thirteen years back
He trod, aft of that red-black
Funnel, down deck after deck

Of Tourist cabins to surprise :
A girl waiting, champagne, goodbyes
Drunk from two tooth-glasses ? . . .

Now it's Pacific, the water.
Above, blades thrash and clatter.
Beside him the seat-belt holds her

Who has held him, whom he has held.
This too is a parting. They head
— With much that may stay unsaid —

To this island, to Avalon,
Close, alone, an afternoon
Before that London plane.

In between, God knows what. Well –
Flats, deaths, jobs, travel,
A marriage and its debacle,

A basset-hound's whole lifetime,
A million words to his name.
Then, kindness waved from

The gangplank. Now, landing steps,
And out to a white-wood township's
Bay-circling steep slopes

Till, by eucalyptus at
The sea's edge they hear – 't 't –
The tiny, sweet-toned ratchet

As humming-birds sparkle, soar
Green up sun-excited air ;
Hand in hand gaze down clear

Water round tall sea-trees, which
Tingles with the golden flash
Of quick Garibaldi fish.

Green bubbles in gold air, then
Gold bubbles in sea's green :
A world of champagne

In a bay-sized goblet
– To celebrate what ?
Love and regret.

On an X-ray Photograph
of the Poet's Skull

1

Strangely light, a filigree
Layered with what must be
Pale lamination.
A brain capacity more
Than appears through flesh and hair ;
Not too weak a chin.

Not like the preconceived
Symmetrically curved
Symbol — solid, white.
A gibber like an ape's
That the dead seem dopes
Sometimes, looks right.

2

Strange, first of all, like myth : a
Setpiece, stylised portrait
Of some minor being of legend,
Blur-masked for what must be the
— As yet —
Not too appalling cold of Elfland.

3

A ' gibber ' ? No, more like a grin
To outface the spot we're in.
The Jolly Roger ! All the fun
Of a dance to the music of
Horror rather than love.
Let the full-toothed rictus prove

We still have time to find the
Rhythm, the accepting gaiety.
But you'd need, to hold that smile,
Hard training. So — not for a while.

4

Above all, how strange the bone-being looks !
One's seen (in Robert Heinlein's books
For example) the notion of the alien ' sleeper '
In the human body, ready to take over.

— These miscalculated. Clearly the plan
Would be to let the fleshy form of man
Disintegrate, when the calcite android
Could emerge, to be reactivated.

In the graves, reserves to master Earth
Lay, confident in their own human's death ;
But the force-patterns to replace muscles failed
In the rare stress of our magnetic field.

In their vigil, immobilised, they lie
To greet the great ships darkening the sky.
But Altair V, the signal unsent,
Has long since written off the whole contingent.

5

An object like a rock or rose ?
— Coolness we can't achieve !
But let's be better braced than those
Whose skull is on their sleeve.

The wild beasts can't be choosers
And innocently unknow ;
It's these obsessed life-losers
That spoil their own show :

Animal again, snarling, foaming — less
Painful, perhaps, if they'd given a miss
To consciousness, or self-consciousness.

Stuck on their skulls, pity each twisted feature
— The bitten lips of the dishuman creature
Crazed with the bad news from the future.

6

The more one looks
The harder it grows :
The grip of its teeth,
The hypnotic blaze
Of its empty orbits.

Behind it a land
Grows coldly visible,
Silicon-scabbed,
With fumaroles drooling
A sulphurous smoke.

Outside, the green
Vitalities sway,
Sentience flies
Or swims the bright streams . . .

But under this gaze,
In a ponderous light
The abstractions freeze.

7

A shell of mind ? But
The black dog hunts bones. Cave canem !
— The backbone connected to the neckbone,
The neckbone connected to the skullbone
And the skullbone connected to — what ?
— The summum bonum ?
Ah, if that were known !

8

It brings too much fantasy
And too much reality !
Everything about it seems quite
Strange, or totally trite.

For once not whistling in the dark (the blinding
Light of knowledge or ignorance made complete),
I hold a brief and probing sample
Of this region with its alien microclimate :
Chart or silhouette of a nice simple
Memento mori. — But who needs reminding ?

As it Comes

I stand in this universe
Seeking completenesses
Without great success.

I meet pretty feminists.
I hear strange erotic boasts.
I see (sometimes) breasts.

But to co-ordinate
Such into group or set
Passes my wit.

And that's only sex ! Add
All the odd, myriad
Cosmic bits — and you'd

Surely agree with me :
Watch out for *category* !
Feeling that can't be

Fully ' conceptualized '
Of sun, poem (OK, breast !),
Tends to be best.

— The trouble with theory
Is that you're hungry
A half-hour later.
One thingburger, Waiter !

In Memory

The last notes of a unique
Voice ran by the dusked fir
Five years all but a week
Ago. Bones of the inner ear

Bore music and meaning, (those two
Alleged contraries, alleged
Complements), sieved through
No metaphored, imaged

Confusion, but clear as that cool
Vista, full as the globed cloud,
Particular as one pine-needle.
— Yet vocalization had

Imposed on the molecules
Of air between a profound
Interweaving pulse
Complex almost beyond

Wave-analysis. And how
(Framed in also appropriate
Elegiac sundown and winged bough)
Could such turn absolute

Those never-again-to-be-met
Harmonies of heart, cries
Of completion, where the straight
Fir frames now emptiness ?

One Way To Look At It

The huge aches they may pant beneath
Should not make poets grind their teeth,
Nor herd into the structured line
The panics of the rooting swine.
Terror and filth subsumed in verse
Must not fall back as shriek or curse :
Unvital and discharging rant,
The lazy egoism of cant.

The cipher of a broken speech
Leaves much beyond the infant's reach,
For language of the fullest themes
Is not disrupted into screams.
— The Greeks excluding from the stage
The squalid orgasms of that rage,
The essence of the bloody hand
Struck generalized, yet still more grand.

Women, knowledge, landscape, art
Make the good elations start.

With these for power the verse may thrust
Strength on the politics of lust ;
View with, not blindness but contempt,
The stinking bilges of the dreamt ;
Till, all proportions manifest,
All high potentials starred and stressed,
Consumately impersonal
Life clangs through art, one lambent bell.

Breathings

Caught in the long wind, draperies
Are lifted, white, round longings. The girl cries,

' Realize me, wind ! Take me, Time ! Pour ! '
Oh how thirsty, in that sweet thirst for

— What ? For life ? No, rather a folding of
Every leaf, every petal, all love

In the unephemeral, the divine. Wind
Of the warm discontent . . . But that other kind,

Frosty, through rasped chiton, envenomed blouse,
Sets in. Sour women fall from the boughs.

A M a t t e r o f D e g r e e

The ice-thick blasts assault and shock.
We inch — exhausted, cold —
Up so refractory a rock
Our pitons scarcely hold.

The black North Face falls from us sheer
Into the mists below ;
With one long overhang to clear
To reach the rich plateau.

Till, sprawled where mind and body break
Exhaustion's last extreme,
We gaze down where, across the lake,
The gold pavilions gleam.

Small figures stroll about that isle,
Snug sheepskin on their back :
Travellers of another style
Who took the southern track,

Borne on those mules they've loosed at last
To crop the clovered slope,
Up paths hacked from the gorge-side karst,
Plank bridges hung from rope.

Mere tourists ! How they'll beam and boast
About their breathless climb.
But what's our profit, who have faced
Forced draughts of the sublime ?

— Tempered to take such last lone treks
As somewhere lie ahead,
We tramp down, bowed beneath our packs,
To food and bath and bed.

In Memory of Lionel Trilling

What weaker disciplines shall bind
What lesser doctors now protect,
The sweetness of the intellect,
The honey of the hive of mind ?

Similitude

He thought of himself as a widower.
It seemed as though his wife had died
And an alien in her likeness tried
Hard to pass itself off as her.

—Unsuccessfully, on the whole,
Lacking enough knowledge of *Homo
Sapiens*' stance, or its eyes' glow,
Let alone adjuncts like heart, soul.

Difficult to prove to a judge,
Unless by a transfer of venue
To a court on Aldebaran II . . .
His fourth Scotch went down like sludge.

Clichés

He said " You mean the world to me. "
   She asked " Do you include
The fruit and corn, the soil and sea
And Ceres and Persephone
And even old grandmother Gé
   And all her endless brood

Of all the living things that be :
   —The elephant and deer,
Seal and beaver, ant and bee,
And dog and cat, and louse and flea . . .
But don't lets take an inventory
   Of all the biosphere !

—The ice that's coldly clenched (and she
   Shuddered) about the Pole,
The storm that shreds up ship and tree,
The fires that fling the magma free,
The strata grinding into scree,
   The reeking oil and coal ?

' World ' in the broader sense ? We see
   The endless parsecs fall
Through cosmic cloud and galaxy
—But let's forget totality
Because, compared with you and me,
   It hardly counts at all. "

Walk That Way

" To flatter beauty's ignorant ear "
Was how Yeats thought he and Catullus were
   Whipped up to the wild verses.

But now we flatter ignorant eyes
Of a deafer lot whose microscope plies
 Through the prints of the poetry presses.

Beauty at least was its own entrée
To the art — a sort of complimentary
 Ticket to the mind's high places.

While in their Departments, trying to explain,
They deconstruct the love and the pain
 Into some sodding great thesis.

Beauties can't, but then nor can dons
Decide what's to be more lasting than bronze :
 And there's not much bronze around these days.

On the Streets

Four or five blocks out of the Tenderloin
I see under neon-fizz as I pay my taxi
A tart, you'd say around seventeen, sixteen,
Blonde, black-hosed, one leg outstretched to lean
Against a lamp-post — a Forties movie scene.
 She looks both sexy and unsexy.

To me, that is. Externals ! But how to judge
What exists, what feels, behind this epi-
sode from La Ronde ? Across the grey sound-stage
Over a presentation of strobed cleavage
Slit skirt, lip-rouge, our eyes briefly engage.
 And she looks neither happy nor unhappy.

Paul Valéry's 'Genoa Night'
(October 4/5, 1892)

At first just stormwaters pouring
Down cobbles of a canted town
To the glaucous heave of the sea.
Prone on the bed he feels faintly
Distant flicker of lightning,
Subliminal thunder-purr.

His life has passed through a swarm
Of demoralizings — as (he'd say)
Earth runs through the Leonids :
The lost girl, the lost aims.
Reasons for not publishing :
Pride, fatigue, foul galleys,
Twisted to one skein.
Non-completion of self.
Egoism ? The end of egoism ?
The brute powers close in.

2

He's weak when the sky slams
Down, blinding, reverberant,
And the whole world, through the whole night,
Unspeakably blares and blazes :
Icy purities of lightning,
Hot savageries of thunder.
A huge inexpressiveness.
He is numb. He is nothing ;
Unlanguaged, unminded.
Clenched teeth, arched spine,
Crouched hour after hour.
It blasts through closed eyelids.
Nagaikas of lightning
Lash at a bared heart.
White-hot pincers of lightning
Pluck at a raw conscience.
Long hoes of lightning
Break up the clods of thought.

And thunder — a huge blind golem
Whose mindless blows thud down
Missing his essence by inches :
His will pounded to powder,
Mind rasped in a hyperaesthesia,
Senses torn from the self . . .

Gored on tines of lightning,
Stunned or not, a concentration.
The beams of the sky break
And the world crushes his chest.

3

A hard mind to crack . . .
But silenced for ten years now
He'll seek through intellection
Poetry devoid of ideas :
Uneveness the worst evil,
Chance accomplishing everything.

' At each terrible moment of history
Some man sits in a corner
Stringing beads ' : in Attila's time,
Or Genseric's, or our own,
In a corner chewing hexameters . . .

Cramped extremes of reason :
Arithmetica universalis.
But beyond rigour — charm.

A cosmos all compulsion ?
But the mind needs for image
Materialities : salt, rose . . .
The storm slowly unravels.
Faint sunrise streams westwards.
And now he turns to endure
Sleep of exhaustion. But the springs click.
The warped wood of the sill whimpers.

Honeymoon in Honduras

Soaked in sweat
In the hot, wet
Mayan November,
Up the steep side
Of that pyramid
She watched him clamber

And pose at the top
To give her a snap.
Back in Maine they knew
It was all a waste
— Overexposed :
The marriage too.

Contact

To walk the dog and myself, in a long day's
Drive, we're pulled over on the hard shoulder
By wire against which tumbleweed
Lies stacked by the wind.
I muse vaguely on women's ways.
— Sub-desert — cactus, creosote bushes — beyond.
We're ten miles out of Carson City,
Far off the Sierra's bleak East slopes smoulder ,
And, squatting twenty yards away, a coyote.
The basset hound stops dead.

Each gives the other
    — Close in origin,
    Apart in experience —
                            a long look,
    Without expression,
    With significance.
Strange concatenation : but I'm struck
With catching it elsewhere, just the other day.
The coyote trots off. We drive away.

The Beach-boy's Song

Sun-scatter from the salt-plumed pool
Fills out your face, my honey ;
And sometimes it looks beautiful,
And sometimes it looks funny.

The tinted shreds of day have set,
Smooth moonlight brims the bay full ;
And sometimes you're so passionate,
And sometimes you're so playful.

And which of them's the ' real you ' ?
Sweetheart, I don't have a clue.

The Other World

The river spins a sleekness through the bridge
And over it a curious figure leans
Pointing his walking stick like a crossed crutch
Into the pearly air and at the streams.

Close to the motionless willows and the cloudless sky
Struggles a world of water, flecked with trout,
And confusion of his images will neither die
Nor even absorb doubt.

He trembles more violently than his reflection,
Frightened not so much at the thought of defeat
Seen in this blue world's surface and cross-section
As for reasons he cannot repeat.

For here it comes : higher than obelisked duty
The flames spout from a heart turned red-hot coal
Yet cannot singe that loose, indifferent beauty
Nor scorify the bilges of his soul.

So on he goes : through solid walls of nature
He walks like a ghost as visions blank his eyes,
Who will never find clear thought or sexual pleasure
Or be able to distinguish poems from lies.

A Georgia Graduation

Four hundred boys and girls — the girls in white
Gowns and mortar boards, a charming sight.
My stepdaughter sways up to take her scroll.
The valedictorian's speech now : from her lips
The innocent clichés fall
In a hushed hall.

Later, by blossomless dogwood, high cypress,
We sit heavy with green darkness
Where fireflies' intermittent, unflickering gold,
Silent as ourselves, sways and dips,
Cool innocence taking hold
Of a hushed world.

Bagpipes at the Biltmore
(Air : 'Strathfiddich ' .)

Downtown Los Angeles :
In the huge baroque lobby
Like the hall of a station
Three men with kilts on,
Skian-dhus and sporrans
And all the adornments,
Stamp round in circles.
One bangs a drum and
The others play bagpipes.

What on earth are they up to ?
And who are the people
Marching behind them
With badges and name-tags ?
An occasional banner :
'U B E W ' —
' United ' , for certain,
' Brotherhood ' , surely,
And W's ' Workers ' .
What about ' E ' , then ?
' Electrical ' , maybe ?
But what has the Union
To do with bagpipes ?
And why are they here in
The bourgeois old Biltmore ?

It's terribly noisy
But fairly inspiriting
— Except, I remember
How we marched as recruits through
The fog-frozen Lothians
With pipers before us :
An ear-splitting torment
Till two brave English laddies
Put paid to the nuisance
With a long knitting-needle,
And the fights and the uproar
Around the old squad-room . . .

My highland great-grandsires
— Macandrew, Macpherson —
Though they much preferred Mozart,
Passed down an old story
Of the head of a septlet
In a bare granite hovel
He miscalled a castle.
After plenty of skirlings
His hereditary piper
With a tattered old plaid on
Would cry to the cardinal
Points of the compass,

' The MacShagbag of Shagbag
Has started to dine.
The Kings of the Airth
May now take their seats ' .

— For that you need bagpipes.
Mere whisky won't do it.
So they do have their virtues,
At least of nostalgia.
But instilling a spirit
In Electrical Workers
To march round the lobby
Of the stuffy old Biltmore
I believe it, since I see it . . .

Just one more blow from
The unreasoned, untidy
World we inhabit
Against our assumptions.
Good for you, really :
Shakes up your smugness,
Freshens your senses
(In this case your eardrums).
I expect that tomorrow
Will turn up with something,
Though perhaps a bit subtler
Than this too sharp reminder
To haul off from habit
And struggle with structure,
With a noise so enormous
I can bellow unnoticed
(And it's pleasant to do it
In the solemn old Biltmore),
' Oh belt up, you buggers ! '

Transpolar

All that ice (he said)
Isn't as cold or hard
As this girl's heart.

Still heading north
We'd flown over smooth
White mile after mile with

Treacherous leads. Now
What stretched out below
Was gouged, scraped, raw

In high clenchings, clamped
With torsion, humped
To blunted fangs, cold-grimed

Nearer black than green :
Above all, alien.
— Pretty bad, then.

It started an argument.
We all said he went
Too far. But we knew what he meant.

Second Death

A ten-pound Life will give you every fact
— Facts that he'd hoped his friends would not rehearse
To an intent posterity which lacked
Nothing of moment, since it had his verse.

Or so he thought. But now we come to read
What his more honest prudence had held in :
Tasteless compulsion into trivial deed,
A squalor more outrageous than the sin.

Piss on that grave where lies the weakly carnal ? . . .
— Hopeless repentance had washed clean his name,
His virtue's strength insistent on a shame
Past all the brief bravados full and final.
Without excuses now, to the Eternal,
He makes the small, true offering of his fame.

Pont des Arts

(On the left the Institut, seat of the Académie; on the right the Louvre.)

A :   The small bridge arcs in air under the dusk
      —That higher arc. What reds ! What turquoises !
      The town, part accident, part artifact,
      Marginally basking, smoulders pale.
      A pale Seine parts those halls of art and language.
      Swifts skim . . . All's still : not tranquil, which applies
      Only to that girl who leans against the rail
      With half-shut eyes. Not tranquil, only still.

B :   Still ? While in Louvre and Institut
          The abstract forges roar :
      Steel for grids to grip and shape
      Loose skies and vaguer cities, or
          For blades to slice them through !

C :   Arced too, her back, her thighs.
      She gazes, grey-eyed,
      Into the grey glide.

A :   Taken for granted, utterly grotesque,
      Lives blaze or sputter in the little rooms
      Behind oblongs of glass, now lighting up.
      — The hunt for rhythm may fail all melody :
      Who has not sat, high in a little room,
      Wrung dry and hollow with a press of love ?
      As your girl there may remind us. All the same
      She's one small vortex among skies and words.

B :   What though the great perspectives plunge
          Or great affections burst ?
      Flame-green theory, jewel of frost
      Can orchestrate the mind-and-heart
          To the hard baton's lunge !

C :   Sex, bút her strangeness too :
      To modulate and drive
      The heartbeat's carrier-wave.

A :   There's shredded cirrus, moon a blank lead disc . . .
      But ' mind and heart ' ? What sort of orchestra ?
      A few strings of a strad, a tom-tom beat,
      Reeds matured or cracked by various weathers,
      As strange and disparate as that moon, those birds,
      The Châtelet's gargoyles, ochres of the air.
      Stone-muted stream ! Regime of accident !
      – Your rigour fails the inexhaustible.

B :   Your weak light drips, your hollow sky
          Is full of beaks and bones
      Unless the mind, the visual cones
      Direct the modes the spectra gleam,
          The curves the phyla fly.

C :   Eyes squeezed to focus ? Better blind
      With a magnesium flare,
      With her lips, with her hair.

A :   The tip of that nilotic obelisk
      May seem to trail high scrawls of indigo
      Limning some glyph upon the tropopause
      – That's no more than the seizing of our eye.
      All speech implies philosophy or song ?
      Yet there, more tritely, the Ile de la Cité
      Cannot but echo in the skull's hard caverns
      As ' a grey frigate breasting the grey waves ' . . .

B :   Art's wildernesses ! Lion shapes
          Steam off its sodden ground
      – Which sharp zarebas can surround,
      Strict pruning bring to symmetry
          The ovoids of its grapes.

C :   The worlds ferment, the words freeze.
      A way to the warm and clear ?
      Through her, here.

A :   Pigments of static iris, marble mask !
      The inexplicit arts that seem to make
      The foliage of detail one green smear
      Somehow accumulate fresh immanence.
      Can words be carved like the great Melian breasts ?
      All thrashing fiercely in our neurons' mesh,
      Phenomena no less than those two barns.
      — Yet see them loom there, nudes, philosophies !

B :   To that great gaze of art and thought
          I turn an equal gaze :
      Striking till planes of fracture crack
      And all essential emerald blaze,
          I'll learn. I'll not be taught.

C :   Tsunami up that total beach
      She waits in art, and for speech
          . . . . *Mademoiselle.*

B :   Rhythmless melody ?

A :   Extreme crystal ?
      And what of the sensuous skeins, the will
      Hammering its harder task ?

B :   Mere explorer's risk ?
      Bright-miraged sand and empty flask,
      Kayak ripped by narwhal tusk ?

A :   Darkness falls on it all.
      The answers ? Well, at least we learn to ask.

The Lively Arts

Their constant cry
Was ' Never say die ! '
Which they're dead
Without having said.

Circumstance

The feminine ways
Of A — poised in grace
By the turret-banked Thames
Or else smart and snappy,
Shading an eye
From the sun, drinking Pimms.

Pure gold. Till he saw
In that waterfront bar
B's brassy display,
Like a caricature,
Malicious and sure
Of the good art of A.

When he met A once more
On the path to the bower
Some portcullis had shut.
He knew it unfair
— But even her hair
Was of similar cut.

They went separate ways.
He could not know that A's
Small gestures, quick smile,
She had modelled on B
— Picked crumbling scree
For ramparts of style.

The Peninsula

Like a finger pointing northward, San Francisco for its nail,
Set between blue Bay and Ocean flecked with white by spray and sail :

Coyote Creek to Candlestick, Pacifica to Santa Cruz
Run the coasts that hold its counties concentrated for the muse.

California soft and mild ! Surely just as fit a nurse
As any rugged Scottish moorland for the child that's into verse ?

Let him grasp our air and landscape, just emerging to the day :
Sunrise runs, one glorious ash-blonde, surfing into Half Moon Bay,

Over Millbrae and San Bruno, San Mateo, Burlingame,
Strung along the old Camino where the Spanish Fathers came.

— Stretches of the old Camino don't recall their mission bells :
Used car lots and drive-in movies, massage parlours and motels.

Never mind — and, while confessing there's a purpose each fulfils,
Two miles East you're in the marshlands, two miles West you're in the hills,

Heading through the open country where the Foothills Freeway swings :
Long lakes glitter under pine-trees, San Andreas, Crystal Springs.

Sun that bronzes without burning, air that's always fresh delights
Woodside and Portola Valley, Los Altos Hills and Sharon Heights.

Easy driving, easy parking, easy shopping, night and day,
In Los Gatos, Cupertino, Santa Clara, San Jose.

Yet there's NASA's installation, looming over Moffet Field,
Our Linear Accelerator with its record muon yield.

For we're not in some Arcadia, work is hard and minds are keen.
Lotus no — but abalone, meunière or amandine,

Washed down by some dry white vintage Santa Clara's hills produce :
Green vines — Novitiate, Gemello, Woodside, Ridge and David Bruce . . .

What's this restlessness we feel, then, where life runs so free and fair ?
Like some instinct to migration thick on land and sea and air :

(Grey whales offshore by the dozen, heading for some Baja cove,
Monarch butterflies in millions swarming to Pacific Grove . . .)

— In Redwood City, Palo Alto, Mountain View and Menlo Park
Some faint tremor warns obscurely from the deep inhuman dark :

Far down, grinding through the magma, Nature brews her huge assault,
And that rift we hardly notice marks the San Andreas Fault.

Winter Welcome to a West Texan

So here you are, lovely :
Arroyos of Kensington
With pekes for coyotes,
Green street-lamp saguaros,
Swirls of fog twisting
Like sidewinders over
The desert macadam.
High boots keep the slush out
As they kept off the cactus
In this English December
     Of a coldish year.

Such high-stepping heels, then,
Such eyes deep-horizoned,
What can she give us
Who has London lassoed and
Corralled and hog-tied ?
— A locus of laughter,
A good supple brightness
By pavements and lime-trees
With their ice-film sheer as
Ten denier stockings
     When the vapours clear.

She brings us the sunshine
Instead ? Not exactly :
She holds her own climate,
Heat, not heat's prickling,
Sand, not its rasping,
No bare, sun-stunned ranges,
Shade without scorpions,
And no Gila monsters
But humming-birds sipping
Flowers of the desert. . . .
    Thank you my dear.

So sun's how it strikes you ?
Then we in our turn feel
Cold, not its judder,
Snow soft on our faces,
December undarkened :
In a jacket as warm as
A sleek palomino
She treads the rime's crackling
With a high winter vigour
Through fog that sparkles
    Like ginger beer . . .

Air and Water

Sassafras, Wye, Chester, Choptank,
Spread rivers of the Eastern Shore,
Are sunken valleys, lawned to the bank.
It's the Tred Avon we're heading for

Down lanes white-aldered, river-birched,
In my side-pocket today's mail ;
I take out a card when the ferry's reached,
And read it, grasping the damp rail.

From a poet : ' I liked your last book
— All about aeroplanes and girls ' .
I photograph her against the wake
That fizzes across those slow green swirls.

Background of oyster-stakes, soft light, low
Crab-boats, high skein of distant geese.
Her form's curved to the rich flow,
Eyes glow, hair lifts to the warm breeze :

Their colours not consciously recalled,
Just suffused through my life's lens.
The boat scuffs the pier now, oaken, old :
I'll do without the aeroplanes.

Kennedy Center

After the concert I
Get a great hearty
Kiss from the mezzo. She's
Big, blonde. What energies !

Still lively after singing
Like the Colorado swinging
Through the ornate hall's
High canyon walls.

Such a magnanimous, calm
Air, too, as she pats my arm,
Sitting in the restaurant bar
To the TV's coarse encore :

A ' group ' — girls mike-in-hand
And looming there behind
A battery of devices
To boost their voices.

What's she got that they haven't
— Apart from voice and talent ?
Instead of the sour
Forced frenzy, a power

Reined under rule
By as strong a rationale . . .
Somewhere in the pit
Of the stomach's where *they* hit

— That is, if they hit at all ;
Many would find the howl
Of a coyote-more moving,
More musical, no less loving :

Their sobs are suggestive
But not sexy, except if
Your ears are wired to your sex
So that it's mere reflex.

So let's get back to the mood
I started in, to the good,
To passionate control :
Where she hits is the soul.

O u t l a w s

' Maiden ! a nameless life I lead,
    A nameless death I'll die ;
The fiend whose lantern lights the mead
    Were better mate than I ! '

She thinks, Oh just a macho stance
    By old Sir Walter Scott,
Yet feels ridiculous romance
    Run through her, sweet and hot.

So complicated, real life !
    All shifting shades are there ;
But welcome, even to a wife,
    The spotlight's simple glare !

She muses on men pure and rash,
    Distilled to fauns or fiends
(More stylish than the toothsome trash
    In women's magazines).

She looks hard at the one she's got
    With love and sense of loss,
Thinking that maybe Lady Scott
    Stood for her share of dross.

Late Pass

The dying animal, one fears,
    Will take us when it goes :
This beast composed of nose and ears,
Legs, belly, heart, and blood and tears,
Will only last a few more years
    And then turn up its toes.

— A mansion that contains its own
    Self-demolition squad :
Brick by brick and stone by stone,
Vein by vein and bone by bone
Till finally the very throne
    Of reason gets the nod.

As we approach that rendezvous
    There's not much we can add
To dicta of the sages who
Gave, as they shuffled up the queue,
Much that is tried, and may be true,
    — At least, the best they had.

So what's our contribution if
    It's all been said before ?
A change of tone's all we can give
Such as that the alternative
Of having aeons more to live
    Might be a bloody bore.

So if our years at board and bed
    Were pretty much enjoyed,
Close the account while we're ahead,
Next year we might be in the red ;
So just forget about the Med :
    Strike out into the void !

And if we feasted cheerlessly
    We still must pay the bill,
When all the consolation we
Can find is that at last we're free,
Home from the sodding awful sea,
    Home from the fucking hill.

So

The poem, calm,
Stands in the eye of the storm,
At most ruffled a bit
By stray residuals of breeze.

The poem, grim,
Is caught in the eye of the storm,
A world's deep, seething pit
Of dungeoning darknesses.

The poem, firm,
Sees with the eye of the storm,
Up and out through the starlit
Perspective of infinities.

Appendix: from REASONABLE RHYMES
by Ted Pauker

Progress

There was a great Marxist called Lenin
Who did two or three million men in
     – That's a lot to have done in-
     But where he did one in
That grand Marxist Stalin did ten in.

A Trifle for Trafalgar Day
(with acknowledgments to G. K. C.)

' Drake . . . Cabot . . . challenge . . . opportunity . . .
courage . . . ' – *The Prime Minister.*

Who's the Dover-based day tripper
       Heir to, Heath ?
– The captain of the close-rigged clipper ?
       Is he, Heath ?
(While for plump young brokers preening
    On the day that Britain joins
' Rigging ' has another meaning
    And a ' clipper ' is for coins . . .)
Was the cry of Drake and Raleigh,
    Tacked into the tempest's teeth,
' Ah, thank God, at last – there's Calais ! '
       Was it, Heath ?

Belgian bureaucrats in boardrooms
       Differ, Heath,
From midshipmites in Nelson's wardrooms,
       Don't they, Heath ?

But would the *Victory* quite suit your
    Grand adventures where they range,
When the Wave is of the Future
    And the Winds are those of Change ?
Though Industry is advantageous
    Ask Sir Alec, ask Sir Keith,
Are its Captains so Courageous ?
                Are they, Heath ?

You'll be needing loyal comrades,
              Won't you, Heath ?
— It's years since Germans came on bomb-raids,
              Ain't it, Heath ?
The red fool-fury of the Seine now
    Has not raged since Sixty-eight.
In Rome for one whole British reign now
    Mere millions cheer the Total State
While in the countries of our cousins,
    Bowed our lousy laws beneath,
Revolutions come in dozens,
              Don't they, Heath ?

Nowadays what does ' The Horn '
              Conjure, Heath ?
Lorry-loads of Danish porn,
              Trader Heath ?
Economic blizzards raving
    Where the frozen assets clot
Are conditions you'll be braving
    Just like Frobisher or Scott. . . ?
No, talk of profit and debenture
    Fix Liège with loans from Leith,
But the Spirit of Adventure . . .
              Chuck it, Heath !

Garland for a Propagandist
(*Air : The Vicar of Bray*)

In good old Stalin's early days
When terror little harm meant
A zealous commissar I was
And so I got preferment.
I grabbed each peasant and I said
' Can there be something *you* lack ? '
And if he dared to answer ' bread '
I shot him for a kulak.
        For on this rule I will insist
        Because I have the knack, Sir :
        Whichever way its line may twist
        I'll be a Party hack, Sir !

Then Stalin took the Secret Police
And gave it to Yagoda.
Many a Party pulse might cease
But I stayed in good odour.
At all the cases that he brought
I welcomed each confession,
And when he too turned up in court
I attended every session.

When Yezhov took the vacant place
And blood poured out in gallons
Thousands fell in dark disgrace
But I still kept my balance.
I studied, as the Chekists pounced,
The best way to survival
And almost every day denounced
A colleague or a rival.

When Yezhov got it in the neck
(In highly literal fashion)
Beria came at Stalin's beck
To lay a lesser lash on ;
I swore our labour camps were few,
And places folk grew fat in ;
I guessed that Trotsky died of flu
And colic raged at Katyn.

And when things once again grew hot
From Western war-psychosis,
I damned the ' cosmopolitan ' lot
Because of their hook noses.
The Doctors should be shot, I cursed,
As filthy spy-recruiters.
But Stalin chanced to kick off first
— So I cursed their persecutors.

Malenkov, now our Party's head,
Tried out a tack quite new, Sir,
Saying what had never been said
— And so I said it too, Sir :
I boldly cried that clobber and scoff
Should go to the consumer
— But his overthrow soon tipped me off
This was a Right-wing bloomer.

When Khrushchev next came boldly on
Denouncing Stalin's terror,
I saw that what we'd so far done
Had mostly been an error.
My rivals all lay falsely framed
Under the Russian humus
And their innocence I now proclaimed
— Because it was posthùmous.

But Khrushchev guessed his chances wrong
And the present lot took over.
And I saw that though we'd suffered long
At last we were in clover ,
Now Stalin's name I freely blessed,
A bonny, bonny fighter.
— And I told the intellectual West
When it's right to jug a writer.

Now the Collective Leadership
Of Brezhnev and Kosygin
I'll back until some rivals slip
By intricate intrigue in ;
And, if the worst comes to the worst
And they're scragged in the Lubyanka,
I'll see they get as foully cursed
As any Wall Street banker.
  And on this rule I will insist
  Because I have the knack, Sir !
  Whichever way its line may twist
  I'll be a Party hack, Sir !

A Grouchy Good Night to the Academic Year
(with acknowledgments to W.M.P.)

Good night to the year Academic,
It finally crept to a close :
Dry fact about physic and chemic,
Wet drip about people and prose.
Emotion was down to a snivel
And reason was pulped to a pap,
Sociologists droning out drivel
And critics all croaking out crap.
For any such doctrine is preachable
In our tolerant Temple of Thought
Where lads that are largely unteachable
Learn subjects that cannot to be taught.

Good night to the Session — portentous
Inside the Vice-Chancellor's gown,
The personage who'll represent us
To Public and Party and Crown.
By enthusing for nitwitted novelty
He wheedles the moment'ry Great,
And at influence-dinner or grovel-tea
Further worsens the whims of the State.
So it is that, however much *we* rage,
The glibber of heart and of tongue
Build ladders to reach a life-peerage
From the buzz-sawed-up brains of the young.

Good night to the Session — the Chaplain,
Progressive and Ritualist too,
Who refers to the role of the apple in
Eden as ' under review ' .
When the whole situation has ripened
Of his temporal hopes these are chief :
A notable increase in stipend,
And the right to abandon belief.
Meanwhile, his sermons : ' The Wafer —
Is it really the Presence of God ? '
' Is the Pill or the French Letter Safer ? '
And, ' Does the Biretta look Mod ? '

Good night to the Session — what Art meant,
Or Science, no longer seemed plain,
But our new Education Department
Confuses confusion again.
' Those *teach* who can't *do* ' runs the dictum,
But for some even that's out of reach :
They can't even teach — so they've picked 'em
To teach other people to teach.
Then alas for the next generation,
For the pots fairly crackle with thorn.
Where psychology meets education
A terrible bullshit is born.

Good night to the Session — the students
So eager to put us all right,
Whose conceit might have taken a few dents
But that ploughing's no longer polite ;
So the essays drop round us in torrents
Of jargon a mouldering mound,
All worrying weakly at Lawrence,
All drearily pounding at Pound ;
And their knowledge would get them through no test
On Ghana or Greece or Vietnam,
.But they've mugged up enough for a Protest
— An easyish form of exam.

Good night to the Session — so solemn,
' Truth ' and 'Freedom ' their crusader crests,
One hardly knows quite what to call 'em
These children with beards or with breasts.
When from State or parental Golcondas
Treasure trickles to such little boys
They spend it on reefers and Hondas
— That is, upon sweeties and toys ;
While girls of delicious proportions
Are thronging the Clinic's front stair,
Some of them seeking abortions
And some a psychiatrist's care.

Good night to the Session — the politics,
So noisy, and nagging, and null.
You can tell how the time-bomb of Folly ticks
By applying your ear to their skull ;
Of course, that is only a metaphor,
But they have their metaphors too,
'Such as ' Fascist ' , that's hardly the better for
Being used of a liberal and Jew
— The Prof. of Applied Aeronautics,
For failing such students as try,
With LSD lapping their cortex,
To fub up a fresh way to fly.

Good night to the Session — the Union :
The speeches with epigram packed,
So high upon phatic communion,
So low upon logic and fact.
(Those epigrams ? — Oh well, at any rate
By now we're all quite reconciled
To a version that's vastly degenerate
From the Greek, via Voltaire and Wilde.)
Then the bold resolutions devoted
To the praise of a party or state
In *this* context most obviously noted
For its zeal in destroying debate.

Good night to the Session — the sculpture :
A jelly containing a clock ;
Where they say, ' From the way that you gulped you're
Therapeutically thrilled by the shock ! '
— It's the Shock of, alas, Recognition
At what's yearly presented as new
Since first seen at Duchamps' exhibition
' Des Maudits ' , in Nineteen-O-Two.
But let's go along to the Happening,
Where an artist can really unwind,
Stuff like ' Rapists should not take the rap ' penning
In gamboge on a model's behind.

Good night to the Session — a later
Will come — and the freshmen we'll get !
Their pretensions will be even greater,
Their qualifications worse yet.
— But don't be too deeply depressible
At obtuseness aflame for applause ;
The louts that are loudest in decibel
Melt away in post-graduate thaws.
Don't succumb to an anger unreasoned !
Most students are charming, and bright ;
And even some dons are quite decent . . .
But good night to the Session, good night !